PRAY

Participant's Handbook

RICHARD J. HUELSMAN, S.J.

PAULIST PRESS
New York, N.Y./Ramsey, N.J.

Library of Congress
Catalog Card Number: 76-24449

ISBN: 0-0891-1976-5

Published by Paulist Press
Editorial Office: 1865 Broadway, N.Y., N.Y. 10023
Business Office: 545 Island Road, Ramsey, N.J. 07446

Printed and bound in the
United States of America

CONTENTS

PRAY

WELCOME TO *PRAY!*

PRAY is a course
>   that underlines the heart of the Christian message and
>   teaches you how to pray over it.

It offers you a plan to put life's pieces together,
>   improve your relationship with the Lord,
>   and grow in His friendship.

It offers support against future shock,
>   ways to love God and others, do some good, and
>   leave the world a little better
>   than you found it.

If you are hungry for God,
>   and desirous to make Him more room in your life—

WELCOME

People are entitled to pray in ways that suit them best.
Early in the program we propose styles, forms and directions
>   that have proven helpful to others.
>   They may prove helpful to you.

Those who complete the course seem to pray better,
>   more easily and more frequently.

They seem to find more meaning in life,
    and feel closer to God, their fellow humans,
    and those with whom they shared the course.

Each meeting is rich and full.
If you must miss one, make up its content through a friend.

Though it invites you to reach for the stars, it is
    built to be gentle and understanding
    towards all who, for one reason or another, want to try,
        but aren't sure,
    or because of duty and the pressures of life
        have limited time to devote to prayer.

    Of course, as with many things in life:
        the more you put in
        the more you take out.

WHAT IS
PRAY

PRAY is a course in how to pray and follow Jesus. It is an
   introduction to selected elements of the Spiritual Life designed
   for good but busy people, to help them grow in love for God
      and others. It is an introduction that spills over
         into practical Christian living.

There is a one-hour meeting every two weeks, fifteen in all,
   Fall through Spring, with time off at Christmas and Easter.

At each meeting ten topics for private meditations are presented,
   along with instructions in prayer, questions, discussion,
      and sharing. It can be offered to individuals or
         groups—large or small.

Participants are asked to spend at least some time alone with God
   between meetings—the amount to be set by each for himself or herself.
      Ten quarter-hours are suggested for the fourteen days,
         an amount which may easily be trimmed or expanded.

People use *PRAY* (make the meditations) in all sorts of ways—
   including while practicing yoga, soaking for arthritis,
      locking themselves in the bathroom for a few moments of privacy,
         early in the morning in bed or over coffee, and even by
            making five at a sitting so "That's that" for the week.

PRAY is intended for adult education at parish or school, as follow-up
   for retreatants, for between-meeting prayer for Charismatics and

3

Cursillistas, for CCD teachers, young Religious,
Third Orders, Christian Life Communities
and more mature students.

It is easy to start and can be guided by priests, sisters or laymen.
It is Scripturally oriented, easy to administer, gentle in its
approach and rich in its content. It is based on Scripture
and early parts of the *Spiritual Exercises* of St. Ignatius.

In short
PRAY aims to be a gentle, enriching, and enjoyable way to learn
to pray and follow Jesus.

MEETING
1
COMMUNICATING WITH GOD—AND—LOVING YOURSELF

Meditations 1-3 are about praying.

1. Getting Ready. "Prepare the way of the Lord." *Matthew 3:3*

For today's meditation:
Read the Introduction to *PRAY*—slowly and thoughtfully.
Talk briefly with the Lord, in your own words,
about why you enrolled in the course, or
about anything else that happens to strike you.
    Ask His blessing.
Decide on a time and place of quiet for praying,
and obtain a Bible, Old Testament and New, in recent translation.

---

2. What is Prayer? "When you pray, say: "Father. . . ."" *Luke 11:2*

Prayer (personal prayer) is communicating with God:
conversing, loving, relating to Him who
    loves us and is our Father,
talking of one's plans, hopes, frustrations,
anxieties, ideals, temptations . . . . holding
    nothing back.
We can also talk about the people in our lives,
about our times, about society,
and above all about Himself, His own wondrous Self,
and all He has said and done.

Communicating however is a two-way street.
At times we will have to learn to grow quiet and listen.

5

To meditate, read "What is Prayer?" again, thoughtfully,
two or three times. Then reflect:
We can talk with God so easily and at any time. No appointment is
needed. Thank Him for the privilege.
Periods of such prayer could mean much for
your life. How?

---

3. **How to Pray.** "Whenever you pray . . . . go to your room. . . ." *Matthew 6:6*

a) To begin a period of prayer, relax, and open yourself to His presence. Become consciously aware: He is near, and cares about you and what you are about to do.

b) Slow down! Read slowly, aloud if possible, pronouncing the words. Think about what you are reading—about each sentence—about words and phrases. For practice, try "one word with each breath."

c) How long should you pray? As long as comfortable. Start with just a few minutes. Even one will do. Mull over the topic during the day.

d) Immediately after reading, try to grow quiet and "listen." What part of the passage attracted you? Go back and savor it, repeat it, turn it over in your mind several times. What interior response does it suggest? Linger over such portions as long as profitable.

e) Sometimes one can't find any meaning. This is not unusual. Try reading again and concentrating on a word or phrase. Try asking questions. Try taking the passage as if it is directed straight to yourself. If nothing helps, move on.

f) Use your own words. As you read notice your thoughts and feelings and talk with the Lord about them. For instance, "Lord, I'm glad . . . . or sorry . . . . or wondering. . . ."

For today's meditation: first
fix the above directions in mind.

Then try them out, one at a time, on
Matthew 6:6:

"Whenever you pray,
go to your room,
close your door,
and pray to your Father in private. . . ."

Meditations Four through Nine say:
God loves you: You are worth much!
(So love yourself!)

---

4. God's Care

Read *Isaiah 43:1-2*
or this quotation from Fr. Trese:*

God does not lose sight of us, as you or I might lose
sight of one drop of water in the vastness of the ocean.
Because of His infinity, numbers mean nothing to God.

If you were the sole survivor in an atomic war,
God could not love you more personally than He does.
At every moment, you have His complete attention,
His undivided love. At this very instant, God is
thinking of you, "looking at" you directly,
loving you.

He is intensely aware of your present problem.
He cares tremendously about what happens to you.
Out of your present burden,
imposed by the ignorance or malice of others
(or your own foolishness)
God is going to bring good to you.

—*Fr. Trese*

For this and the following meditations, use the directions given in 3 above.

5. God's Plan

God has created me
to do Him some definite service.
He has committed some work to me
which He has not committed to another.
I have my mission.
I may never know what it is in this life.
But I shall be told in the next.
I am a link in a chain,
a bond of connection between persons.

He has not created me for nothing.
I shall do good. I shall do His work.

Therefore, I will trust Him.
Whatever, wherever I am, I cannot be thrown away.
If I am in sickness, my sickness may serve Him.
If I am in sorrow, my sorrow may serve Him.
He does nothing in vain. He knows what He is about.

He may take away my friends, He may throw me among strangers,
He may make me feel desolate, make my spirits sink,
Hide my future from me—
Still He knows what He is about.

—*John Henry Cardinal Newman*

6. God's Goodness "With age-old love I have loved you. . . ." *Jeremiah 31, 3*

Consider all the good and all the love God and others have poured out on you since your earliest years. Start with childhood.

Make a list of the talents, good times, love and friendships, etc. you have enjoyed. Which do you value most? Consider not only benefits from God but from the many fine people you have known. How much they have done for you! For all you have received how will you ever thank them—or Him?

7. Your Own Goodness

Consider how many beautiful and how many loving things *you* have done for God and other persons all through these years. Of which are you especially proud? Was any period of your life unusually rich in such accomplishments or love? Whatever good you've done will never be lost: will be to your credit forever and ever.

For all the opportunities, the abilities and His inspiration to do it all— thank Him. Ask help to be generous in pouring out the great goodness within you.

8. Your Sufferings

Consider the sufferings, disappointments, illnesses, struggles and failures you have been through. Have you borne any of them rather well, all things considered? Congratulations! Which were most painful or cost you most? Who or what supported you in these difficult times?

Though God doesn't exempt us from the human
condition—including suffering—He is willing
to stand with us, to be with us all the way.
Ask for His comfort and strength.

9. Your Sins

Consider the faults, sins, bad example, hurtful words, meanness and wrongdoing you are responsible for in different periods of your life. It may not be easy to admit them. Which do you most regret?

Consider: In spite of these neither God nor persons have given up on you. He never will. You have everlasting indestructible value in His eyes. You are worth so very much. (Why?)

Thank Him and pray for those who have stuck with you. Thank Him especially for His forgiveness . . . and for theirs.

---

10. Prayer for Success and Generosity

Reread the Prayer Instructions in Meditation 3.
Then talk with the Lord about your hopes
    for success in prayer this year.
What prayer-efforts have you made thus far in your life?
    With what results? What are you looking and hoping for?

Remember that God loves you and is eager to communicate.
But on your part there is nothing so helpful to progress as a generous
    heart, one eager to reach out and seek Him, one eager to
        "See Thee more clearly,
        love Thee more dearly, and
        follow Thee more nearly . . ."

    Pray for this, for the members of your group,
    and for your spiritual guide. Conclude by
    reading Psalm 103 (102) in praise of God's
    goodness, or Psalm 63 (62) 1-9 longing for God.

Friend: One who knows all about you, and loves you just the same.
—*St. Augustine*

2

LIFE HAS A PURPOSE

Meditations

1. My Purpose in Life

God is our Father.
He created us
to share His life, His goodness, and His love with us
in His Kingdom—now and forever.

He invites us to share these gifts more and more fully—by becoming
persons who love Him with all our minds, and hearts,
and souls and strength,
and our neighbors as ourselves,
that "His Kingdom may come."

So to live through all the years,
in good times and bad, in work, prayer, everything—
that's my purpose.
That's how Jesus lived. He'll be with me.

This is an important meditation. Try to be as deeply
convinced of it as you possibly can.
Allow yourself to feel the peace, joy, and sense of meaning
it brings to life.

Then read Mark 12:28-34a to see these thoughts in Jesus'
words. (Kingdom: the reign of God, His reign of love.)

2. God

a) Who is He? Who or what is He like? What was your predominant image of Him during childhood? Adolescence? What is it now? "For me God is. . . ."

b) What are the names or titles for God you like best? If you had to select your favorite, which would it be? Why?

c) Compare yourself with God. Which of you is greater, wiser, stronger, more loving, and how much so? (Which of you is infinite?!) How are you similar and dissimilar in the ways you think and act?

Then stand humbly in His presence—indeed, in awe—and talk of what you think or feel.

Finish your meditation with a prayerful reading of Psalm 103 (102) 1-13.

---

3. Created—I am Created. Reflect:

I am created. Once I didn't even exist—was nothing—sheer nothingness—like a dot that continues to shrink until there's—*Nothing!* (Stand humbly in His presence for a while and think: What shall I say—I who am Nothing—to Him who is Everything?)

Then read Genesis 2:7 and think how fortunate you are to have been given: Life! Try to get the imaginative feel of it as if, like the first person, you just realized: "I'm alive! I exist."

What does it make you feel like saying to the Lord?

---

4. Created from Love

Read Isaiah 49:14-16. (Repeat the verses several times.)
Reflect that you were created because God wanted *you* in particular, and no one else would do. He is your Father.
You are His son or daughter.

Pour out your mind and heart, or,
simply remain quiet for awhile, letting yourself
experience the sense that you are loved just *as*
you are—that "God is very fond of you."

---

5. Prayer Experience. Praise of God.

Besides all He has given in Creation,
our Father has shown still more love
by His call to each of us to be a Christian.
Each of us, and each in a very special way, is one
of His own chosen people.

This privilege is well described in 1 Peter 2:9;
and is foreshadowed in Deuteronomy 7:6-8.
Read both of these texts as if directed to yourself.

Then look around at all His other wondrous gifts:
sea, sky and nature; body, mind and soul . . . .
How many they are!

Let your heart expand at the sight and sing
praises as you feel inclined. (Use Psalm 150
if you like.)

---

6. Loving God with "all one's heart. . . ."

Life is no brief candle to me;
It is a sort of splendid torch
Which I have got hold of for the moment.
And I want to make it burn as brightly as
possible before handing it on to future
generations.

—*George Bernard Shaw*

How does one "burn brightly?"
What would you like to leave
to future generations?

---

7. **Pain and Suffering:** an Invitation to Trust in God's Love for You.

Ordinarily, God will not exempt anyone from the human condition, which includes struggle, pain and suffering. He did not exempt His own Son. However, if we let Him, He will help us bear them and turn them into good—in the long run, that is, and in the total picture of His plans— though these plans be hidden from us—for here we are involved in a mystery.

And if He does not seem to answer our prayers the way we think He ought, it will be helpful to remember that He is a saving God; and He is wiser than we are. We'll understand in due season. "God does not play dice with the universe."—*Albert Einstein*

Were your sufferings ever blessings in disguise?
Has your trust had its ups and downs?
Through your sufferings, is there something He wants
you to learn? (*See Hebrews 12:7-13*)

---

8. **Jesus' Purpose: His Father's Will**

For Jesus, the All-Important Thing in life was:
to do His Father's will. Read Matthew 6:10, and 12:46-50; John 4:31-34.

How can we know His will? We can know it from thinking and praying about signs found in Scripture, Jesus' life, Church teachings, one's talents and personal limitations, duties and the circumstances of one's life, practices of good people, good advice, and above all: conscience.

For most, to live by God's will in even the small
things of life would represent dramatic change.
If you'd be willing to say: "I'll try, Lord, to do
whatever you like," what do you think He would say?

---

9. One Day at a Time

A good start at trying to follow God's will in everyday life comes simply from asking: "Taking life as I find it, what should I be doing here and now—today? I may not know what tomorrow will bring, but what does the Lord want me to do, suffer, or enjoy—today? Who does He want me to try to help, put up with, or forgive, or what kind of person should I be trying to become—today? (What's my task in life—today?)

Try to do this as well as you can, with all the love and enthusiasm you can muster. At the end of the day you'll know: You have Done Your Best. No one can do more.

> To meditate, read Colossians 3:23-24 and see yourself doing this at different times during the day: "Here's an hour for you, Lord. I hope you like it."

---

10. An Application

Read the First Meditation again and reflect: What would it
be like—how would it feel—if you were trying to live by it
in your own special way a typical day?

One author puts it this way:
> To awaken each morning with a smile brightening my face;
> To greet the day with reverence for the opportunities
>   it contains;
> To approach my work with a clean mind;

To hold ever before me even in the doing of little things
   the Ultimate Purpose toward which I am working;
To meet men and women with laughter on my lips and love
   in my heart;
To be gentle, kind and courteous, through all the hours;
To approach the night with weariness that ever woos sleep
   and the joy that comes from work well done—
This is how I desire to waste wisely my days. —T. Dekker
   (How would you see *yourself* doing it?)

A PRAYER INSTRUCTION
(Read occasionally)

1. To set the stage: Relax. Seek an atmosphere of peace and quiet. (Pretend a Doctor ordered it and see what measures you'd take.) Put aside other concerns and become aware: He is dwelling within you; He loves you—just as you are. Let yourself rest in that love for as long as you wish. He is eager to communicate and cares about what you are doing.

2. Helpful to meditation:

    a) a set time and place;

    b) pre-reading: reading over the meditation before retiring so it can "germinate" before you actually meditate;

    c) an attitude that prayer is important—that your meditation period is special—something you look forward to;

    d) reading something—prayers, Psalms, or spiritual reading just before meditating. For some, a picture or crucifix helps set the mood. And why not a hymn or a song?

    e) reading the text aloud;

    f) reading the text as if it is directed to yourself.

3. After reading, pause to "listen." Open yourself to simply letting the passage, text, or the Lord, "work" on you. Grow still and try to become aware of your "deep down" response to what you have read. Let that interior response lead to expression in prayer—converse with the Lord about whatever your response may be.

---

4. After listening and responding as moved, for as long as you desire, you may wish to:
   a) Think about the passage or topic in His presence, analyze it, apply it to life.
   b) Talk with the Lord about it. Try to get a feel for really meaning what you say.
   c) Praise, thank, ask, express sorrow or some other emotion.
   d) Quietly wait even longer for some other interior response—thought, feeling, or inclination-to-act—to occur.

   All of these are good prayer.

---

5. If you need help for reflection: ask questions, make comparisons, or look for relationships: What is Jesus saying? What does this incident remind you of? How would you apply it to your life?

---

6. Linger over insights, phrases or parts of a text that attract you.

---

7. At the end of your meditation pause for a moment of more intimate conversation with the Lord, or the Father or His Spirit.

8. Feel free to express all feelings in prayer with reverent frankness, even negative ones like fear or aversion as well as positive ones like joy or praise.

9. If it helps praying, one may walk, stand, kneel or lie down. Some are helped very much by beginning their prayer in a posture of reverence. (One may also float in a pool, listen to music, surf, ski or gaze at the stars.) If you find what you want in one position do not pass to another. Likewise if you find what you want in a particular thought, emotion or resolution—or there find closeness to God—do not pass to another.

10. Really meaning what you say in prayer is more important than how long you pray. Without enough length, however, deep prayer may not occur. Aim for the length that suits you best. Push yourself longer occasionally. You may be surprised. Try to be faithful even if periods are short. A minute a day is worth more than an hour a month.

If you are exceptionally busy try at least to read the meditations, and then continue to mull over them during the day. This is recommended for longer meditations as well. If one or another of the meditations is particularly helpful, it would be good to spend an extra day or two on it— you be the judge. Notice the title of the meditation and of the meeting itself. The title can help focus your reflections.

MEETING

3

EVERYTHING HAS A PURPOSE
EVERYTHING IS A GIFT, OR AT LEAST AN OPPORTUNITY,
TO LOVE AND SERVE THE LORD

Consider the advantages of each meditation. They invite us to generosity—to love as our Father has loved.

1. What Things Are For

Everything has some good use. It is—or can be seen as—a way to grow as a person who loves God and others with mind and heart and soul and strength.

Everything—all things—
joys, blessings, worries and hurts—
friends and neighbors, family and work, praying and playing—
health, money and youth, or lack of all three—
struggles, illnesses, and the circumstances of life—
    are all gifts or opportunities
    for growing in love.

To use all things for this as well as one can,
to make changes or lay them aside when they hinder,
this is wise usage, good stewardship.

This is a profoundly faith-filled view of life.
What would it mean if you took it seriously?

2. Talents and Crosses.

A steward is a manager or administrator—one to whom something is given in trust.

We are stewards of our gifts and talents—and our crosses too.
With them we can love, do good, and bring
others and ourselves to happiness and fulfillment
in our Father's Kingdom, here and hereafter.

At this point in your life:
What is your finest talent or your biggest cross?
Are you doing any good with it—or in spite of it—on a typical day?

---

3. "Barns" and Using One's Money. Read Luke 12:13-34

Look around. How many people do you see making really good use of
their money? What is the best use you could design for your own,
if you really put your mind to it, with both generosity and
good sense? What would be the advantages?

And to reflect still more deeply:
What would you do if you lost what you have?
How much do you really need?
Is what you have a blessing? Is what you don't have a curse?
Should everyone be rich? (How poor is Christian?)
If you suddenly inherited a million dollars,
how would you decide what to do with it?

---

4. The Poor

Read Matthew 25:31-46. A powerful text! We need not go far to find
those in need. The sick with many burdens, the hungry for love, the poor
in body or soul—persons somehow in need of care or help—are all
around. We can love close to home.

Those in need aren't always the "nicest" to deal with.
But that is not the point of the reading. (Or is it?)
Talk with the Lord as moved.

5. The People in My Life

The Lord has given me some care over—some responsibility to shepherd or steward—all with whom I live, work or study, my family, friends, neighbors, fellow workers. I am—to some degree—responsible for their morale, attitudes, what they think or talk about, and perhaps even how they feel about God, Christ or religion.

Am I my brother or sister's keeper? Read Genesis 4:8-10.
I am. Should I also be everyone's friend?

Consider how well you are relating with those with whom you live or work closely.

6. Why Should We Love?

Read and note the point common to the following: Matthew Ch. 6:1-20; Ch. 10:42 and Ch. 16:27. (See also 1 Corinthians 3:8; and Ephesians 6:7-8)

By loving God and others more now, we increase our capacity to love Him and others more intensely hereafter. We also increase our capacity to enjoy their love for us. "One added degree of eternal happiness is worth all the sufferings of this world." (St. Theresa.) Does the thought urge you to try to become more loving? Should a Christian be working for greater eternal reward? Isn't that selfish? (Why did Jesus say it?)

7. Success and Happiness

These motivate most people. What are your ideas about each?
One definition: Ultimately one is a success to the degree
that he or she has helped as many as possible to the greatest possible sharing in God's grace and eternal reward.
Another: Ultimately one can be called a success to the degree

that he or she has become a certain kind of person—rich in love, Christlike, noble.

Are these the same? Is one better? (Feel free to argue.)

And happiness—what is Happiness?

Happiness is that good feeling in one's heart when (when what?)

Browse through Matthew Ch 5, 6 and 7. Any clues?

(See Matthew 5:3-12. Does *that* sound like happiness? Do you think it would *feel* like it?)

For meditations 8-9-10:
If you prefer, review a former meditation
or use the Alternate (below.)

8. The World's Resources

The future belongs to those who lay claim by molding it.

Read Genesis 1:26-29. Then consider:

God put us into the world to shepherd and cultivate its resources.

We are here to manage and thus serve the needs of all.

"Use everything to love." We are here to use things, not to amass them.

This implies that we should not waste, misuse or hoard the (limited) resources of our planet to the unloving harm of others.

Each of us must start at home; consider this and talk with the Lord.

---

9. Position of Influence

Read 2 Samuel 11:1-27. (David took unfair advantage of his position.) As you see "big" people at work today, think: who are making best use of their influence, power and position?

Could you make any better use of your own?
By your gentle encouragement could you help anyone
grow, prosper, flourish or just come out of his or her
shell? Could you effect good for your business,
school, America, your friends . . . . anyone at all?
(But what if you are on the lowest rung?)

---

10. Charisms of Personality and Good Looks

If one is especially good-looking, athletic or brilliant, how does he or she keep from becoming a show-off or "pushy"? If one is very plain-looking and easily lost in the crowd, how does one avoid becoming catty, lonely, over-eating and "trying to get attention"? Should I be cultivating good grooming or gracious manners a little more? Do I worry too much about how I look? Is anyone any better for my gifts? How can I make the most of who I am?

(For thinking:) Pope John was old (77), bald, short, fat, had a large nose, big ears, and was starting to die of stomach cancer when elected as an interim Pope—"til a real Pope could be found." With all this "against him" as it would seem, what did he do: invest in hair pieces and plastic surgery, or withdraw and give up? No, he just went ahead to become one of the best-loved and most highly respected people in all the world! (There must be something I can learn from this!)

To stimulate further thinking, read Ezechiel 16:1-43 and 36:25-29. Why is the Lord so hard on Israel?

An Alternate Meditation. Recreation. The Father likes to see His children happy. Consider how much time, energy and money you spend on recreation and how much good comes of it. Even time "wasted" now and then can be quite Christian—but anything can be carried to excess. For a beautiful Scripture reading about apportioning time, see Ecclesiastes 3:1-8.

All that is needed for the triumph of evil, is for good people to do . . . . nothing. —*Edmund Burke*

TIPS ON MEDITATING (SOME OLD, SOME NEW)
(*Re-read occasionally*)

1. When learning to pray, pray as long as inclined. If the periods are very short, lengthen occasionally. For longer periods of prayer, ten or fifteen minutes is ordinarily a minimum; twenty or so minutes often works better. First unwind. Then recall: He is dwelling within. You may communicate with Him there. Rest in His presence, then ask His help to pray well.

2. After reading a text: "listen" interiorly for a time, and communicate with God in any way that you feel drawn. After that, if you wish, make use of reflection, feelings, and/or choices and resolutions—as inclined. Or make acts of praise or request, or just rest in His presence.

3. To Stir up food for reflection about a text, try any of the following:

   a) Ask questions. Who? What? Why? Where? How? Does it Matter?
   b) Note relationships: How is this connected with Jesus, our destiny, something we believe in, some feeling, something or someone important, a choice to be made?
   c) Make a comparison. This reminds me of . . . is like . . . is quite different from. . . .
   d) Refer the text directly to yourself; or to the nation; to the present or future; to people you know, or to everyday living.
   e) Notice feelings: feeling hopeful, loving, thankful, worried, afraid, hurt, satisfied, critical, confident, happy, confused, depressed, dry, elated, empty. All are food for prayer. Notice especially feelings of resistance. Where do they come from? What do they mean?
   f) Think and pray about the meaning of important words: "Blessed," "Messiah," "Shepherd."

4. Scripture. Sometimes it is more profitable to meditate over a whole passage. Sometimes over just a word, phrase, or sentence. Read the passage

through, then decide. Don't rush. One idea can change your life!

5. It is sometimes helpful to read a passage *aloud*, even several times. Try emphasizing different words or phrases with each reading.

6. Sometimes the best topic for meditation is your most pressing problem, joy, or sorrow. If it weighs heavily on your mind: "If you can't lick 'em, join 'em."

7. Encourage occasional prayer-contacts with God during the day. One can pray about almost anything: one's family, business, parish, a current event, movie, newspaper account, song, the dawn, a friend, a humorous saying, a slogan.

8. If easily distracted, copy out the Scripture passage slowly in writing. (This forces attention.) You can also write or vocalize your thoughts while meditating. Some people draw.

9. Be natural. Talk to Our Lord or Blessed Mother like a friend, in your own words.

10. If one or another meditation doesn't turn you on, take another, or review one you liked, or design one of your own. Don't try to use all the above directions at once. But re-read them occasionally and use as helpful.

11. When pressed for time: read and run; but continue to mull over the topic during the day.

The meditations of this meeting, though challenging, are meant to cast a kindly glow about life by pointing out how everything—every least thing one has or owns, and circumstances such as being young or old, or having a hard life or an easy one—can be oriented towards greater love. Absolutely everything can have meaning—even eternal meaning. We need only accept life, people and ourselves as we find them and try to respond as Christians. We need only to take one step at a time, one day at a time, and not be discouraged at failure. We need only to try. And knowing that we are loved every step of the way helps. It brings Hope, and Joy. He has shown us the Way.

Note that the ideals here proposed will be lived differently by different people. Thus, not every person is called to live in actual poverty as a witness to Jesus. But some are, and perhaps more than we think. Many certainly need to think about moderating their life-style as an aid to greater love; and everyone is called to develop a very Christian attitude toward money. In many cases, the decisions involved will rest ultimately on the depth of one's generosity. In other cases, circumstances, the needs of others, one's talents and abilities, or one's position in life may be decisive factors. Each must ask: What would the Lord like of *me*? Regardless of what others may be doing, what would He like of me? What kind of person and what kind of response is He looking for in *me*?

In these matters people are different. To use a homespun comparison: like horses, some need the spur, some the rein and some just to be spoken to gently.

For some persons: Go man, Go! Adjust those priorities! You can find time for prayer . . . . if you really want to. You can be a Christ-bearer in your own way too. It's all a matter of motivation. If things are difficult, more effort and less excuses! You can learn! And remember, you are not an owner of what you possess, only a caretaker. The world needs your help. And God asks for it. He has called; He will help.

For others: Easy does it. Don't strain. And don't feel guilty about not doing enough. The Lord is inviting you to reasonable effort and the good news is that

He counts your very efforts as success! Go gently. One day at a time. And discouragement is simply "Not Allowed!" Remember: He loves you.

To still others: Are there obstacles to Love, and to prayer, in your life—perhaps sufferings of mind or body or heart? (Do you ask: Why Suffering? And Does He really hear?) Or may it be a strain in human relations with a loved one? An economic insecurity? Feeling one is not loved or doesn't amount to anything? Could consulting a spiritual guide, counselor or physician, or somehow rearranging one's life-style or expectations of oneself—or others—bring about more peace? Perhaps these, along with prayer and reflection, might be the winning combination.

The Problems of Suffering—A Reflection for Moderns
(*Optional*)

Sometimes people feel deeply distressed:
They wonder: How can God allow such Terrible Things to happen to innocent people? Is Anyone Out There? Does He hear Me? Does He Care? These and other thoughts nag at the spirit and make it difficult to pray, or to love "with all one's heart."

If you are one of these, ask for grace to take the "leap of faith," put your hand firmly in His in trust that, if you do not see the way, He does.

Such darkness is not unusual among Christians—and that includes the saints. It might be consoling to read the autobiography of the Little Flower, St. Therese of Lisieux. She too, towards the end of her life suffered greatly from such trials, wondering if there was a God, but decided to trust in the power of Love.

Perhaps the following will help:

> "Einstein once made the remark to the effect that God is subtle but not malicious. We have difficulty understanding His designs, not because He places obstacles in our way; but because their beauty and intelligibility strain our capacities to their limit. But we are meant to understand, and

29

with His help we do so more and more as time and history move toward the far distant day when what we may hope for no longer remains a question." *America*, March 30, 1974, "The Second Coming and the Cosmos."

In other words, what the problem of suffering shows is not that God is evil, but that I with my little intelligence, my little mind, am not all that smart. Why—I don't even know why grass is green!

Oh, sure I do. Grass is green because it contains chlorophyll. Why does chlorophyll make it green? Well, because—among all the wave-lengths combined in common white light, only the green is reflected by the chlorophyll; all the rest is absorbed. Why is all the rest absorbed? Well, because the molecular structure of chlorophyll allows it to absorb all but the green which it then reflects. Why does such and such a molecular structure absorb the rest but reflect green? Well—ah—you see—well, we just don't know, I suppose (why grass is green!). He knows. He is wise. Trust Him. He is a saving God. Thus he stands portrayed in both Old Testament and New, incapable of causing evil or suffering for their own sake. But since they exist He must have some reason to permit them. Suffering and evil we believe are the result of man's misuse of freedom. Somehow even all of nature is involved, though why is a mystery.

Further, even the Lord did not explain the "whys" of the problem of suffering. But what He did do is: He showed us how to live with it, how to turn it toward something of meaning and good, and sent His Son to show Who had power over it. That however, is much—and much to be thankful for.

We believe that in the over-all picture—the long-range and global view— He will help us draw good even from evil and suffering. If we cooperate with Him, He will help us find meaning and benefit in our misfortune. He will be with us to comfort, strengthen and at times heal.

MEETING

4

OBSTACLES TO LOVE: SIN AND
SELF-CENTEREDNESS. "REPENT . . ."

Meditations

1. A Reflection on Our Times

Stand at a busy street corner, and look into the faces of those passing by.
The world is far from being filled with persons who love God,
love others, and long for the Kingdom. Many feel empty,
unhappy, and "lost"
as they rush through life
seeking mostly comforts, money, importance,
to be loved or admired at any cost, power over others
or just to have a good time.

Many become unfaithful in marriage,
neglect God, disregard law and authority,
cheat or steal, practice discrimination,
drink too much, endlessly criticize
      but do precious little about it.

Even many good people live everlastingly just for themselves
and what they can get out of life—or get away with—
forgetting:
we are called to be lovers, stewards, and life has a purpose.

Some prefer sex or romance to love,
or pleasure—to anything.
Some escape tensions or boredom with drugs, erotica,
or violent entertainment.
Many are unwilling to reach out to others,
or commit themselves to anyone or anything—

except complete freedom.
And so we see:

Tensions and strife; racial, class, marriage
and personal,
injustice and crimes, violence and wars,
divorce and poverty, insecurity and discouragement,
feelings of powerlessness and guilt, low self-esteem
and insensitivity to the needs of others,
and even to their most basic rights.

Nature is damaged, "love" grows stale, and—
even life—is held cheap.

It's no wonder some people just "withdraw."
We have let our Father down.

How did we ever get this way?
Are we on collision course, or can we go on as we are?

Before we set our hearts on anything too much
let us examine how happy they are who already possess it.

—*François de la Rochefoucauld*

---

2. Examination of Conscience

Go to our Father and ask whether there is something very basic (much deeper than thoughts, words or actions), some disorderly feeling of heart, some misplaced priority, some refusal to accept life on His terms, some tendency to live for *me*, something I don't want to let go of that keeps me from love, and about which I must stand before God with sorrow.

What is there about myself—or the way I live or act—
He would most like me to change?
Why am I so enmeshed in this fault?
What must I do to get free? What is the first step,

the one that will really put the axe to the root?
Be as definite and specific as possible.

To work at a fault in a systematic way:
Take it one day at a time. On arising, *pray* and *resolve*.
Gather strength through motives: by considering advantages
such as growth that would come with the change.

Before retiring, mark down how often you failed: appoint
a symbolic penance; plan (visualize) how to improve for
the morrow.
Compare totals occasionally. Getting anywhere?

---

3. Sin

Read Romans 7:15-24 prayerfully, slowly.
Confront the mystery of sin: Why do I do what I do,
and keep on doing it?
Does sin seem real? Important? (What is His view?)
Review the place sin has in your life, one period
at a time; childhood, adolescence—what you
have done and what you have failed to do.
Do not stir up scruples. You are loved and forgiven (See 1 Timothy 1:15-16)

Talk with the Lord as you feel inclined.

---

4. Prayer Experience. Death.

Time will come when you will know:
Life has about run its course.

Mull over this very profound and human experience
all through the day, even in your busiest hours.
What do you think this realization will be like?

What comfort, human or divine, would you like at
    this time?
See Luke 12:16-21 for a perspective
on sudden death.

---

5. Prayer Experience. Heaven.

Use your imagination. Give free rein.
Make comparisons. Will it be like
    Revelation (Apocalypse) 21:1-27 or 22:1-5?

Yes, your friends will be there.
Yes, there will be action.
What will you be glad of in the forever and ever?

---

6. Sorrow

I have sinned . . . I am sorry . . . for I have neglected or
displeased God . . . been hurtful to myself or others . . .
refused to help others when I could have . . .
neglected so often to follow His lead . . .
and am all too likely to do so again.

And as to "small" sins—though consequences may appear small,
there is a delicacy about a relationship of love, whether with
God or anyone else; and little things—even a bit of coldness—
can make a great difference.

What shall I say?
Read prayerfully Psalm 51(50)
See also Romans 7:24-25 and 8:9-14.

7. The Mercy of God

Read Romans 5:6-11. Or pick some favorite Gospel
passage about the forgiving kindness of our God, such as
the Prodigal Son (Forgiving Father) or Lost Sheep—
both in Luke 15. Note that to forgive—and to be forgiven—
are cause for rejoicing.

> Do you need anyone's forgiveness?
> Does anyone need yours?
> Have you forgiven yourself?

> Praise of His mercy:
> See Psalm 136(135)

8. Examination of Confession

> Has it contributed to *growth* over the
>   past few years?
> Has it been very routine?

Would it help to confess just *one* fault (if there are no serious sins),
    especially some sin of omission that is hindering growth. This one
    fault should be confessed in some detail, and in its causes, and with
    mention of some plan to work at it until next Confession. All briefly.
    Confession should result in healing and growth!

9. Prayer Experience. You at your best.

Lie back.
Dream.
Your ideal self:
> a) What kind of person would you really like to be? (To what is He
>   calling?)

b) How would you—at your best—live a typical day?

What is the *first* step, be it ever so small, to start
actualizing the dream?
(If you are going to start changing, you have to start
somewhere, sometime.)

---

10. **"I Confess"**—sacramentally or in private. Make it one of your best.
Remember: You are meeting—not just the priest—but the Lord.

The following sequence is recommended by spiritual writers:
1. Thanks for God's benefits.
2. Prayer to the Holy Spirit for light . . . and for courage to follow.
3. Examination. How do you most want to grow? What do you most
   need to do? (What would *He* want?)
4. Sorrow. Allow yourself to feel really sorry that . . .
5. Plans for amendment. What's the first step?
   (Let it be something you can check on.)

Appendix "Perplexed Conscience"

In trying to live for God, it is sometimes difficult to know which choices
to make. First consult the ordinary sources: Scripture, Church, counsel
and conscience. Try to make sure you are seeking God's will, not acting
on disguised self-interest. If after that, you still cannot make a decision,
the following quotation may be helpful.

"When you come to a decision on a moral question that is not clear and
simple, but complex and ambiguous, you might in effect, say to yourself:
'There are conflicts in the many voices I have listened to, but this is the
way I see it before God. This may not be the ideal that I want, but the
ideal is not feasible. This may be the less undesirable between two difficult
choices. I will live out my decision as conscientiously as I can. If I am
kidding myself, I ask forgiveness. If something comes up to change my

mind, I will change it. But I have made my decision and I will do the best I can—in honesty before God."

U.S. Catholic—May 1973
from the article "Does the Catholic Church Have the Answers?" by Nelson and Wakin

There is only one Tragedy—Not to be a Saint. *—Leon Bloy*

MEETING

5

PAUSE TO REFRESH

During the next two weeks do whatever you think will most help your progress in prayer. Relax, refresh, review, resolve, or just rest. The important meditation is the first below. Try to get as fully convinced of it as you can—even if it takes a few days. Is there anything about it to which you feel resistance—or which you especially like?

Meditation 1

Review and Summary of our Purpose in Life as Children of God our Father.

God is our Father.
He has created us to share Himself with us in His Kingdom.
He has given us all that we have
      to love Him and serve Him,
      and others as ourselves,
      that His reign of love may come.

Those who want to respond gratefully
try to fill their lives with good works:
giving cups of cold water, forgiving trespasses,
and such others as Scripture commends. See Matthew Ch. 5, 6 and 7.

They try to orient the ordinary:
business, partying, studying, and raising a family,
joys, sorrows, and even the monotonies of life,
in such a way
that they manifest their identity as His children
and speak their love to all.

At best they are fine human beings, deeply sensitive to all
      that is noble, good and best.
Their rule of life is Jesus' own: His Father's will.

They feel basically good about themselves, about people, and about God.
They know that suffering is a mystery—but that it is safe to go on in trust.

They try to be gentle, faithful, honest and patient.
Knowing human weakness, they try also to be compassionate,
    because our Father is compassionate.
They do their best a day at a time,
    to be part of the solution and not part of the problem.
They know the ideals we are studying are challenging,
    but they like challenge. And besides,
    you only live once, why not make the most of it—
        for both worlds?

This world could use more like them.

This (as far as we have gone in our course) is somewhat of a sketch of a
    Christian personality. Write a sketch for yourself.
    (Have we left out anything of importance?)
St. Paul in Colossians 3:12-17 says some of the above in his own way.

Read Matthew Ch. 5, 6, and 7 for a still more detailed sketch—by Jesus.

Meditations 2-10
Review former meditations—especially prayer-directions. Open the Bible at random, make some needed resolutions about prayer time or life-style, try experimenting with meditation in bed (doesn't always work!), take a vacation from prayer if that will refresh you most, or ponder some of the following:

A) *Prayer Experience*

Look up at the stars and pray as moved. "If the stars should appear one night in a thousand years, how men would believe and adore, and preserve for many generations the remembrance of the City of God which had been shown! But every night come out these envoys of beauty, and light the universe with their admonishing smile . . ."
—*Ralph Waldo Emerson*

What are stars for? Response of a seven year old: "Gee, Daddy, God must be Somebody nice to have given us all those shiny things."

B) *Prayer Experience*

Turn on the radio, and make the first thing you hear—into *prayer*. Certain love songs lend themselves to this exceptionally well. Try this as a night prayer.

C) *Difficulty Praying.* Check as possible causes:

1) Physically indisposed, nervous, or tense.
2) Emotional upset, anxiety, deeply hurt feelings. (A worry about health, children or love?)
3) Dry period—one of those ups and downs that go with anything in life. (At times we must wait on the Lord.)
4) Lack of proper place or atmosphere of quiet.
5) Lack of unwinding, proper preparation, or becoming recollected in the presence of God.
6) Need for more time, or more motivation and appreciation for prayer.
7) Lack of method.
8) Doubts about faith.
9) Can't feel right with God because of disorderly attachment to sin, object, person, ambition. . . .
10) Feeling "overburdened" by high ideals, by trying too hard, or discouraged at lack of progress.
11) Not "listening" enough.
    Then—if the difficulty persists, *do something.*
    Re-read the prayer directions in Meetings 1-2-3- and 5.
    Talk with the Lord; then with a friend, physician, counselor, or spiritual guide as appropriate.

D) *Decision*

Consider seeing *PRAY* through to the end—barring the unforeseen. We are about to consider the Kingdom (Meeting 6.) Christmas (7.) Getting to Know Jesus (8-9-10.) Following Jesus in Love (11-12-13.) and Spiritual Growth (14-15.)

MINUTE MEDITATIONS
(*For Enjoyment*)

With a little practice, you will find that, should you have only a few moments, you can pray about just about anything:

About Making Progress: If at first you don't succeed, you are running about average.

About Working: By working faithfully eight hours a day you may eventually get to be a boss and work twelve hours a day. —Source unknown

About Living: Dear Lord, Sometimes I so long to cut through the complexities of modern living and simply love—*love*—just love—and do and be and seek first the Kingdom and sing and dance and be uproariously, ridiculously glad—Because You are *you* and I am *me* and people are *people* and life is *life*, and I love them *all*, and You love *me*—and THANKS!

About Dying: The Master: Do not allow yourself to get discouraged during the dark nights. They are all of them blessings in disguise and as long as you live you must learn to suffer for my sake. So don't let death scare you, for when it comes, I shall give you all the graces you need to accept it in the spirit of Christian hope. Ask again and again for this grace of final perseverance and I will infallibly give it to you. —*R. Kreyche, Making of a Saint*

About People: We must remember that God made man at the end of the week —when He was tired! —*Mark Twain*

About Despair: Never despair. But if you do, work on in despair. Also: If shipwrecked, pray to God and row for the shore. —*Russian Proverb*

About Habits: If you would not be of an angry temper, then, do not feed the habit. Give it nothing to help its increase. Be more quiet at first, and reckon the day in which you have not been angry . . ." I used to be angry every day; then every other day; now every third and fourth day. . . ." And if you miss it so long as thirty days, offer a sacrifice of thanksgiving to the gods. . . .—*Epictetus*

About Praying: Be patient. Prayer life is a growing process. Resolve you'll never give up. Never! And if you do, pray on anyway!

If you haven't time for meditating, at least read the materials. They will keep you in the perspective of the course.

But—"The man who is too busy to pray, is busier than the Lord wants him to be!"

SEVEN POINTERS ON PRAYER
(*Traditional*)

Seven specific suggestions which have been commended by many Christians through the ages:

Pray each day at the same time. No matter how many spontaneous prayers you may offer during the course of the day, you should also have a fixed, regular time for private prayer. Treat it as the most important appointment in your day and don't let anything intrude upon it or crowd it out.

It is helpful to have a regular place as well as a regular time for prayer. It may be a place you find convenient, so long as it affords complete privacy. Jesus recommended a closet. In the modern home or apartment, that might be translated into a bedroom or bathroom. Lock the door, if possible. Your ability to concentrate on your prayers is directly related to your assurance that no one will see, overhear, or interrupt you.

The posture you assume in prayer does not matter to God, but it may make a great difference to you. You can stand, sit, kneel, or lie down to pray. Kneeling is a physical act of humility which helps many people to prepare psychologically for prayer.

Prepare for prayer with a brief period of devotional reading. This helps you to make the transition from the hectic world of daily routine to the quiet mood of prayer. It enables you to focus your attention on God, an act which is both the precondition and the purpose of prayer.

Pray as long as you want to—and no longer. Jesus warned that long-windedness is not a virtue in prayer, and the model prayer he gave to his disciples has only sixty-seven words. Until you are far advanced in the spiritual life, you may find it difficult to sustain a genuine mood of prayer for longer than five or ten minutes at a stretch. It is better to pray briefly and regularly than to indulge in marathon prayers one day and then skip several days.

Pray—whether you "feel like it" or not. Even the most saintly go through frequent "dry periods" when they do not feel the least bit prayerful. But keep on praying.

Do not be ashamed to offer "selfish" prayers, or to seek God's help in "little" things. Jesus included in His model prayer a petition for bread, which is about as mundane a request as you can make. But you shouldn't let personal petitions dominate your prayer. They are likely to do so unless you deliberately practice other kinds.

What other kinds? Spiritual directors have identified four—intercession, confession, thanksgiving, and adoration. Intercession has been described as "loving your neighbor on your knees." This is the prayer in which you seek God's help for other people.

Confession is the prayer in which we acknowledge our sins and accept God's forgiveness. Thanksgiving means counting your blessings. As in the case of intercession and confession, it is always better to be specific—to thank God sincerely for particular good things in your life. Adoration is the highest form of prayer. It means lifting up your heart to God and saying in whatever words you find most meaningful that you acknowledge him to be worthy of your utmost love and obedience.

(Excerpted from *Haircuts and Holiness* by Louis Cassels. With permission of Abingdon Press, Nashville, Tenn.)

MEETING

6

THE GOOD NEWS: THE KINGDOM IS HERE

Meditations 1 and 2 constitute a parable. They ask for response.

Meditations

1. *Parable of the Kingdom* (Part 1) *A Call from the Leader of a Nation*

   See in your mind's eye a great leader, calling his fellow citizens in a time of emergency to help him restore national honor and bring peace, honesty and trust to the nation; to achieve a balanced economy, safe streets, and a renewed interest in religion; to insure that no one is hungry or uncared for.

   He will head the campaign himself and feels sure to succeed. He asks all citizens for all the help they can give, and promises for their efforts and hardships that they will share well in the benefits the new order will bring.

   > What kinds of response is he apt to get?
   > For example, from the generous?
   > Do you think such a call would appeal to you?
   > Is the above realistic? (Feel free to argue.)

2. *Parable of the Kingdom* (Part 2) *Christ's Call*

   See in your mind's eye Jesus, the most just, compassionate, attractive, authoritative, wise and influential person who ever lived.

   See Him inviting all men—by international appeal—to help Him make known and acknowledge His rightful claim to lordship of the world.

   See Him asking all men to help Him bring peace, happiness and love, justice, trust and caring, abundance of life for us all—the poor and underprivileged especially—a life beginning right now and growing to unimaginable fullness forever.

He says He will lead the campaign and feels sure to succeed. But He wants my help—mine personally—all the help I can give. He says He'll reward every effort, every discomfort or hardship endured, and allow me to drink of the fountain of youth—the waters of life—whereby I'll always be young and lovely—the better to enjoy my life with Him and our friends, in a privileged place in His Kingdom, forever. *See Ephesians 1:9-14*

It's really a fantastic offer.
Have many accepted?
What are your own deepest thoughts and feelings
about what to say or to do?
Or how far to go?

(Important for the generous: A sense of joy, elation, and gladness at the call.)

3. *Christ Needs You. He Has No Hands but Yours.*

During the last World War, a bomb-shattered statue of Jesus was refashioned from the scattered fragments by soldiers on leave—all but the hands which they were unable to find.

With both wit and insight one of the rebuilders titled the handless image: "He has no hands but yours."

Does Christ really need us? Why?
You? Me? All kinds?

4. *The Kingdom*

should be marked by:
truth and life
holiness and grace,
justice, love and peace.

—*See Preface for the Feast of Christ the King*

Martin Luther King said it this way in his Nobel Peace Prize Acceptance Speech:

> "I have the audacity to believe that peoples everywhere can have three meals a day for their bodies, education and culture for their minds, and dignity, equality and freedom for their spirits.
>
> I believe that what self-centered men have torn down other-centered men can build up.
>
> I still believe that one day mankind shall bow before the altars of God and be crowned triumphant over war and bloodshed, and non-violent redemptive goodwill will proclaim the rule of the land.
>
> And the lion and the lamb shall lie down together and everyman shall sit under his own vine and fig tree and none shall be afraid. I still believe we shall overcome."

For your meditation, read it aloud, and savor the beauty and grandeur of the vision for awhile.

5. *The Kingdom. Prayer Experience.* Read Isaiah 65:17-25.

Dream your own dream: What would the world be like
(if it were what-it-could-be-like and should-be-like)
if the Kingdom were fully here?
Or what would your neighborhood be like . . . or your home life?

6. *The Kingdom*

Jesus says: (in Matthew Ch. 13 *Read* vv. 18-50 and note:)

1. vv. 44-46—the Kingdom is a treasure worth having at any price.
2. vv. 47-50—but for the time being we'll have to accept the fact that God tolerates evil-doers among those working for it.
3. vv. 18-23—but hang in there in spite of difficulties (!) and you'll bear good fruit.
4. vv. 31-33—even though it seems to come slowly and you don't see

the results of your labors all at once.

What is Jesus telling us here?
Pray over one of the texts.

7. *A Generous Response.* Consider:

Which vocational or occupational roles by their very nature help most to contribute to the Kingdom? (Is that a reason to choose it?) Which ones hinder? What can one do as businessman, wife, etc.?

Which free time and recreational activities can most help contribute to the Kingdom? What of football, records, dancing, music, writing, hiking?

Which courses of study or serious reading can help one contribute? Can the ordinary ones like, oh say—English Lit, Chemistry II, the 6:30 News, *Time, True Romance,* or *Yoga is For You?* How so? (What can I do, Lord? Will it Matter that I Was?)

8. *A Generous Response.* Read 1 Peter 2:9 and reflect?

To be baptized is to be a member of that group which Christ has especially called—we are that royal priesthood, holy nation, chosen race and people set apart of which the Preface sings—to be his agents in establishing the Kingdom among ourselves, our communities, our country and the world. This is a deep and solidly Scriptural notion of what it means to be a Christian. Far more is involved than simply: "Creed, code, and cult."

An excellent start to accomplishing these ideals occurs when we adopt life-styles which include:
  Frequent prayer,
  study, and
  action.

Could almost anyone adopt such a life-style?

9. *Apostolic Prayer Experience.*

Today, consciously and deliberately do something to further the Kingdom. Offer special prayers; or read or study about an issue in which Christ or Christians have a stake; or engage in talk or some action to "leave the world better than you found it." (Anyone who can write, talk, or phone—or just be nice to someone can do something!)

In prayer, plan it; rehearse it mentally;
and see yourself feeling good—feeling joy—about
carrying it out.

10. *The Eternal Kingdom*

The Kingdom of God—His reign of love—begins in this life and comes to full maturity in the next. Everything that we do here matters for the next, will be somehow taken over and transformed. We do not know exactly how, but we know that it will.

It is this hope of the final possession of the everlasting Kingdom—which is the deep and unshakeable joy of the Christian. He knows that eventually all will be well—for He has been redeemed and saved, is precious to and guarded by—the King Himself.

In the eternal Kingdom, what do we look forward to?
Scripture suggests:

Colossians 3:4	We shall appear with Him in glory,
Luke 22:27-30	eating and drinking at His table and judging the Twelve Tribes,
John 17:24	in the company of Jesus glorified
John 15:15	and as His friends;
1 Peter 1:4-7 and	having for our own: an imperishable inheritance which will not fade, and
1 Peter 5:4	which will include praise, honor and glory for ourselves.
1 Cor 15:41-42	Somehow we shall shine like stars
Revelation 21:4	with death and all our illnesses banished forever;

1 Cor 15:42-44	with bodies transformed and wonderfully glorified;
1 John 3:2	and we shall see God as He is
1 Cor 13:12	face to face
Rev 21:1-3	in a home grand and glorious
1 Cor 3:8	where we shall all be rewarded, but
1 Cor 15:41-42	differently befitting our efforts
Eph 6:6-8	and our merits.
Rev 22:12	
Matt 5:19	
Matt 6:19-20	
Matt 10:42	
Matt 16:27	
1 Cor 2:9	So—indeed—"Eye has not seen. . . ."

In your prayer, try to feel the hope and joy of it all.

(Spend what time you can on it now, and
return when you have more.)

MEETING

7

PREPARING FOR JESUS (CHRISTMAS)
ADVENT PRAYER, AND RELIGION IN THE HOME

I. ADVENT PRAYER SUGGESTIONS

Meditations 1-3 are three meditations, based on the Kingdom, about using emotions in prayer.

It is proper and can be quite stimulating to use and dwell on emotions in prayer. These three meditations afford practice.

1. **Interior Kingdom of Prayer;** allow yourself to feel deep peace and contentment at the thought of how you have been nourishing your prayer-life (or intend to:—even during the Christmas rush)—the interior Kingdom of union with God and Jesus. Feel "blissful." Feel "coaxed." Let the feeling of satisfaction about making an effort to pray urge you to want to continue your efforts.

---

2. **"Thy Kingdom Come."** Allow yourself to feel deep peace and contentment at the thought of how you wish during this holiday season to build up Christ's Kingdom of life, truth, grace, holiness, justice, love and peace—His reign of love—by bringing His presence a little more, some way, into your life at home or at work. (Could you be influencing your place of business? school or community?) Let the feeling of satisfaction at how worth-while such activity is "coax" you to want to engage in it.

3. **"The Great Day."** Feel deep peace and contentment at the thought of your good fortune to be a Christian—preparing for His (the King's) coming soon, and preparing by your whole life for the Great Day when you will enter the eternal Kingdom. Enjoy and be thankful: Life *does* have a meaning.

4-10 Other Advent Prayer Suggestions

4. **Your Heroes.** In your prayer, or as you go about during the day, consider your heroes: Do you have any? (Should one?) Are you anyone's (You may well be!) Should one try to be better than he or she just naturally is? (Is that being phony?) Should one "just be oneself?" (Is "being oneself" a Christian ideal?) When you thought of your hero did you think of Jesus Christ?

5. **John the Baptist:** An admirable man. Could we in our times benefit by such as He? What might He say—if He stood at the center of town or some street corner, or in a pulpit, or wrote an editorial? Would anyone listen? Texts for His life-story may be found in Matthew 3:1-12; 11:2-15 and 14:1-12.

6. **Rifts.** Talk with the Lord about healing the rift between yourself and someone else with whom relations are less than cordial. "Cultivate an enemy. He might become a friend."

7. Prayer Experience.

Study and pray over an object, drawing or symbol associated with Christmas (or the Incarnation.) Hold it in your hand. Look at it steadily for some time. Let a new depth of meaning arise from even such a familiar sight as a Christmas tree, banner or greeting card text.

8. Use Advent daily Mass texts for meditation. (See *over.*) Pick out a sentence or phrase and concentrate on it. Or use Advent or Christmas hymns.

9. Scripture. Read Luke Ch. 1 and 2, and talk a great deal with Mary. Or read Isaiah 40:1-11 and/or 42:1-7.

10. Talk with the Lord about "Religion in the Home" (as below.) Or design a meditation for yourself along similar lines.

Some Alternatives:

A) *St. James' Epistle.*
   Read it all at once or a chapter a day. It has much to say about "good works" and the poor. Reflect: It's not wrong that I should have so much—but is it right?

B) *A Good Turn.* Resolve on one. (For example, visit or sing carols for shut-ins or give to the poor.) Decide that if by day's end none has been done, you will say some definite prayers for a worthy intention. Do not retire before saying them—no matter how tired!

C. *Spiritual Reading.*
   Buy and read a book about Christmas, the Old Testament, or the Prophets. Even better: Go to your religious book store and browse.

D. *Penance Experience.*
   Stay a bit hungry through the day. Offer the cravings each time you notice them for (specify your intention.) In this way, you can become partners with Christ in His redemptive suffering. Allow yourself to feel the kind of "pure" joy that comes with this kind of self-discipline—refined, delicate, spiritual pleasure, quite different from that which comes from indulgence.

E. *Poverty Experience.*
   "Let Go" of Something—or Just Do Without—and See What Happens.

F. *Prayer Experience*
   Invent your own personal mantra—a short, prayer-phrase or plea that echoes and rings within your own deepest self. It might be simply the Holy Name. Sing, chant, or just allow it to float mentally all through the day, in the midst even of other activities—whenever you think of it. "Maranatha." "Come Lord Jesus."

G. *Remaking Christmas*
   Reflect: Should we all be trying to make Christmas more "spiritual," and do all the gift-giving some other time?

II. RELIGION IN THE HOME

Topics

1. Good Example

   (a) If children see that parents give prayer a high priority in their own lives, they may be impressed.

   b) Sunday Mass is well prepared for, not rushed. Certainly no leaving of Mass early.

2. Teaching at Home

   a) Establishing attitudes is of highest importance—more important for the very young than doctrinal instruction. For example, respect for life, respect for people.

   b) Children respond more to use of imagination and symbols than to words.

   c) Examination of conscience: How to teach it to pre-schoolers: a positive approach.

   d) Formal Teaching: Take an interest in your children's religion classes; read and discuss their text-book materials with them.

3. Taking Advantage of Teachable (Psychologically Privileged) **Moments.**

   a) All Liturgical Seasons, especially Advent and Christmas, Lent and Easter, and certain Feast Days. Also, First Communion, Baptism, Confirmation, Marriage, Sacrament of the Sick.

   b) Natural events such as birth, death, a personal or family crisis, a crisis in society. Sickness. Also birthdays and special events in the family.

c) Children's questions: Take time; or re-schedule.

---

4. Mealtimes and Family Prayer

a) Conversation at table.

b) Prayer. Also, family religious customs. Repeating efforts toward family prayer that do not at first succeed.

Discussion: Strengthening Family Life.

Possibilities: Family Night—together once a week or month with nothing interfering. Camping. Picnics. Outings. Trips. Projects together. Apostolates.

> REMEMBER: OUR NEXT MEETING IS IN JANUARY
> MERRY CHRISTMAS!

Dec—First Week:

Mon	Isaiah 2:1-5 or 4:2-6 and Matthew 8:5-11
Tues	Isaiah 11:1-10 and Luke 10:21-24
Wed	Isaiah 25:6-10a and Matthew 15:29-37
Thurs	Isaiah 26:1-6 and Matthew 7:21, 24-27
Fri	Isaiah 29:17-24 and Matthew 9:27-31
Sat	Isaiah 30:19-21, 23-26 and Matthew 9:35-10:1, 6-8

Second Week:

Mon	Isaiah 35:1-10 and Luke 5:17-26
Tues	Isaiah 40:1-11 and Matthew 18:12-14
Wed	Isaiah 40:25-31 and Matthew 11:28-30
Thurs	Isaiah 41:13-20 and Matthew 11:11-15
Fri	Isaiah 48:17-19 and Matthew 11:16-19
Sat	Sirach 4:1-4, 9-11 and Matthew 17:10-13

Third Week:

Mon	Numbers 24:2-7, 15-17a and Matthew 21:23-27
Tues	Zephaniah 3:1-2, 9-13 and Matthew 21:28-32
Wed	Isaiah 45:6b-8, 18, 21b-25 and Luke 7:19-23
Thurs	Isaiah 54:1-10 and Luke 7:24-30
Fri	Isaiah 56:1-3a, 6-8 and John 5:33-36

Dec 17	Genesis 49:2, 8-10 and Matthew 1:1-17
Dec 18	Jeremiah 23:5-8 and Matthew 1:18-24
Dec 19	Judges 13:2-7, 24-25a and Luke 1:5-25
Dec 20	Isaiah 7:10-14 and Luke 1:26-38
Dec 21	Song of Solomon 2:8-14 or Zephaniah 3:14-18a and Luke 1:39-45
Dec 22	I Samuel 1:24-28 and Luke 1:46-56
Dec 23	Malachi 3:1-4 and 4:5-6 and Luke 1:57-66
Dec 24	II Samuel 7:1-5, 8b-11, 16 and Luke 1:67-79

On Waking

Dear God,
I thank you,
I worship you,
I love you!

Joyfully,
I offer you this day,
With all it holds for me.

Enable me, this day
To be a better person,
To love and help everyone
I come in contact with,

To participate in
The renewal of the Church
and
The building of a better world.

These things I ask,
In the name of Jesus Christ.
My Lord and Savior.
Amen.

At Close of Day

Dear God,
I thank you
For all your gifts today.

Bless and reward
All who have been kind to me,
Who, helping me,
Have shown their love for you.

I give myself,
And all I love
Into your keeping.

Forgive our sins.
Grant peace and pardon
To all men and nations.

Move people everywhere
To love and help one another
As your children—
That the Church
May be renewed
In Jesus' name.
Amen.

Msgr. Josiah Chatham

8

FINDING JESUS THROUGH THE GOSPEL OF MARK

*Meetings 8, 9 and 10 are intended to help you grow
in a more deeply personal love for . . . Jesus*

Directions:

The plan of each meditation is the same: Each day read one chapter from
Mark's Gospel, beginning at the first. But (optional) just before reading, read a
paragraph in Archbishop Goodier's article, or one from another life of Christ,
to warm the mind and set the tone for reading the chapter in Mark. The
paragraphs need not harmonize with the Chapters in Mark—they are merely
to help set the mind in a reflective mood.

In ten days you'll have the experience of reading in Mark most of the public
life of Christ (Passion excepted.) This overview will be a good prelude to our
next two meetings—also about Jesus.

If you choose to read Goodier or some other author as a warm-up, notice the
personal appreciation that that author found for Jesus from his reading about
Him in Scripture. Goodier's portrait is classical, but its warmth is unmistakable.
More contemporary portraits stress Christ's humanity—his interior struggle,
feelings, etc. The point of this meeting is to suggest that you find *your* own
view, that you read Mark's Gospel as a way to be growing in your *own*
personal appreciation. Who is Jesus to you? What does He mean to you?

When you have finished the chapter in Mark grow quiet and wait for interior
reaction. It may take some little while before you feel moved to respond, but
even such waiting is good prayer. If after a time, something to pray over comes
easily, fine! If not, try asking *no more than one or two* of the following:

Thought Questions

What are your reactions to this passage? If you had to

give a short talk about it, what would you say?

What response was Jesus seeking by what He said or did?

How did Jesus impress the onlookers? How did they react?

How would you apply the passage to yourself? (What message is
the Lord sending for your life?)

A Few Others

What is the most striking characteristic about Jesus
you find in this passage?

Does Jesus still want to do today—somehow—what you
see Him doing here?

What in this passage might apply to everyday life:
eating, drinking, sleeping, dealing with the
neighbors, getting the day's work done?

Does this passage imply that Christians are different
from other people?

How is this passage (chapter) connected with the one preceding?

Why is this passage so important—why do you think it
was chosen to be included as part of God's word?

From this passage can you discern certain values which
guide Jesus' choices?

"I wonder how I would Have felt if I were there?"

Do you feel resistance to any part of the passage—
or strengthened or consoled? Why?

Who is Jesus to you? Does this passage contribute
anything to the way you think about or love Him?

Do you feel a sense of weakness or inability to
respond to the challenge of the
passage? (Say so to the Lord. This could
be a fine beginning for prayer.)

Remember: one or two of the above will ordinarily be enough for a mediation.

END EACH MEDITATION WITH A HEART TO HEART TALK WITH JESUS.

Meditations:

1. Goodier #1 and Mark Ch. 1
2. Goodier #2 and Mark Ch. 2

   etc. for the entire ten days.

   Checkoff: 1 2 3 4 5 6 7 8 9 10

An Alternate Prayer Experience. After reading a chapter, sit. "Do nothing." Just watch and listen. Let come whatever comes as you mentally join the scene, and simply watch, love, and stay in His company.

If nothing gets started,

read part of the chapter again—more slowly—
and pause wherever you find some profit.
Linger as long as it lasts; Or

ask one of the Thought Questions directly of
Jesus—then wait quietly for signs of
interior response. For example, "Dear Lord
what impression would you want this
chapter to make on me—how would you like
it to strike me? Is there something here
you want me to see?"
Let one of the Questions, or the answer, lead
after a time to your expressions of faith,
love, sorrow, joy, fear, doubt, praise—
some human feeling, some response.

The early Christians did not say in dismay:
Look what the world has come to;
but in delight:
Look Who has come to the world!

Note:

Don't worry about passages in Scripture that are obscure; for the time being, draw what you can from those that are clear. A deep knowledge of Scripture requires much study and though useful is not indispensable for prayer.

Meeting Eight—Supplement

1. It is important for us to bear always in mind that we learn Our Lord as He was and, therefore, as He is, wholly from the Gospels. Other Lives of Him, other writings, books of meditation and the like, may help us to interpret Him; they may give us the fruit of the discoveries of others; but in the end even the most inspired and the most living of these must be referred back to the Gospels; if their picture differs from that given by Matthew, Mark, Luke, and John, then however beautiful and fascinating and elevating it may be, it is not Jesus Christ, but some fine fancy of an artist's imagination. On this account, whatever else one may read and study—Lives of Christ, works on the spiritual life, mystical books, the letters and other writings of saints, great biographies, inspiring histories, records of martyrs, sublest theology, annals of the Church, poetry the most sublime—all, it may be written to enlarge and deepen our concept of Our Lord—still one can never lay aside the constant reading of the Gospels; the constant following of Him through their pages Who alone, and in them alone, is set before us infallibly as the Way, the Truth, and the Life.

And, in fact, in them we have enough; not, it is true, enough to satisfy our human curiosity, for we are keen, almost beyond endurance, to know everything that can be known, even to the most trivial detail, about this "most beautiful among the sons of men"; but enough to form a perfect picture, nay more, enough to bring up before us a living reality, the study of which will occupy us all our lives, will occupy all men all their lives, and even at the end the mind will not be exhausted.

2. Let us but look for Him there, allowing other books to help us as they may, but not making them our final source, and we shall find Him for ourselves. We shall find this Man, Jesus, stamped from the beginning with a strange directness and clarity of vision, which nothing can ever divert, or draw aside, or make to falter; He could meet His mother's tears with a direct reply: "Did you not know that I must be about my Father's business?" the remonstrance of John the Baptist, the first of saints, with the check: "Suffer it to be so; for so it becometh us to fulfill all justice." To the end there is never any confusion, any doubtful understanding; He walks through life and death knowing always what would be.

3. We shall find Him next, as a natural concomitant to this, always clear, and firm, and decisive in His judgments, speaking always "as one having authority," always so that His enemies were forced to exclaim: "Never has any man no matter what the circumstances against Him, spoken as this man speaks"; unhesitating, true, no matter how men heckled Him, how they tried "to catch Him in his speech," no matter what tact He was at times compelled to employ.

4. We shall find Him unerring in His estimates of men; He is never deceived or drawn away by a surface impression, never yields unduly, or against His better judgment to occasion, never confounds evil with misfortune; but distinguishes truth from falsehood, real evil from real good, the canker at the root of human life from the mere withered branches, the "things that are for the real peace" of men as opposed to make-believe forms; He discriminates between reality and truth in all alike, whether in the heart of a disciple or in that of an enemy, in the saint or in the sinner, in the believer or the pagan, the conventionally good, those who pass muster among men, or the outcast criminal.

5. This stamp of utter, unerring certainty and of absolute trustworthiness because of certainty, is the first trait we discover. Alongside of this we shall find Him the tenderest of hearts, a father, a mother, a brother, a sister, a true and not a patronizing or condescending friend, the exact equal of each and all, with an individual understanding and sympathy for every heart that opens out before Him, yet never does He confuse one with another, never does He weary of one in preference for another, much less exclude one for the sake of another, never is the love or interest of anyone diminished because He has love for so many. On the other hand, never is He weak, or overindulgent, or soft, or too blinded by affection to see the evil or the limitations of His beloved. He gives love lavishly and to all who will have it, even the most debarred from human love, yet none would call Him languid or sentimental; He wins love from those who are conquered by His presence, because He is so true, so strong, so selfless in purpose, so single-minded, so unable to deceive. Men might call Him by bad names; they might accuse Him of evil deeds; they might say that He worked by Beelzebub, that He was possessed, that He was an imposter, that He blasphemed; they could never say, though He loved so much and showed it, though His love went out to the most loathsome and abhorred so that some took scandal, that this His love was ever other than understanding, and true, and generous, and enduring, and uplifting, and in itself perfect.

6. Again, we shall find Him ever constant. He has a definite work to do, a definite life to live and death to die—that is written on every page of the record in His journeys, in His teaching, in His attitude to men, as much as it is constantly and repeatedly expressed in His words—and never for a moment does He swerve in its accomplishment. Failure may depress Him, but He does not despond; opposition may alter His plan, but it does not slacken His effort; malice does not embitter Him; deceit, falsehood, trickery, deliberate misconstruction of His words or actions, desertion, treacherous friends, faithless or weak-kneed companions, fruitlessness of all He may do, even deliberate rejection—none of these things can lessen His endeavor, make His hand tremble, or the feet on the mountains falter. None of these things can alter Him; always and everywhere, from beginning to end, He is the same; He seems to give no thought to consequences, or fruits, or rewards; whatever the results, He has a work to do, and the doing of the work is all that He considers; He labors, not looking for rewards; toils, not demanding rest; steadily He walks through life to His goal, "giving testimony of the truth," "speaking as one having authority," always "going about doing good," to all alike, deserving and undeserving, friend and enemy, alien and ally, who will deign to accept from Him the blessings He strews along His path as goes.

7. With these three—His absolute truth of understanding, His boundless, tender heart, His constancy in action—we shall find Him, as a necessary consequence, looking out on men with infinitely tender eyes. Never a human being comes within His horizon, but He looks through it with eyes, of accurate judgment it may be, but infinitely tempered by love; with intimate understanding He interprets it, with the welcome of friendship He receives it; there is not a good thought thinkable about it, not a good interpretation possible to put upon its wayward deeds, but that thought and that interpretation will have found a place in His mind. While others find reason justly to condemn, He will find reason to save; while justice puts a limit to the time of repentance, and permits the law to run its course, He will wait till the very last moment, and in the end will rescue. He does not compel men; He has too much regard for them to drive. He offers them Himself and awaits the issue; when they look wistfully He invites them to draw near; once or twice only does He make the first step, usually He leaves that to them; but when they do come near, when they do let Him see that they want Him, then His eyes glisten, and His heart expands, and His hand opens, and there is interest, and sympathy and longing in every look and gesture; He was never so near seeming foolish, as when some pleading soul showed that it believed and responded, and the key was thus applied to the flood-gates of His bursting affection.

8. These are four main lines that go behind the portrait of Him "that cometh from Edom, with dyed garments from Bosra, this beautiful one in his robe, walking in the greatness of his strength," as the four Gospels consistently describe Him. This is He who, when the Evangelist himself endeavors to depict Him in the abstract, can only be summed up in the words of the Prophet: "The bruised reed he shall not break, and smoking flax he shall not extinguish:" yet whom that same Prophet also called "Wonderful, Counsellor, God the Mighty, the Father of the world to come, the Prince of Peace." We see Him clearly enough before us, and we know we are not mistaken: this Man of firm, unflinching manner, yet with not a shadow of hardness; grave in His looks, inspiring silence, yet with it something that attracts; an eye that looks out to long distances, yet not a soul feels itself passed over; glistening as through tears, yet strong as the eye of an eagle; a lip that trembles as the lip of a quivering maiden, yet so firm set that the weakest has courage from its strength. We see Him wrapt in deep thought, speaking words that set the wisest pondering, yet withal in such simplicity that the children understand Him; looking out beyond the limit of life, yet not a flower in the field or a bird of the air, or an outcast cripple on the roadside is forgotten; with a toiler's hand, and brain, and heart, and ambition consumed with eagerness for labor, yet ever ready to yield up His task when His companionship is needed; consumed with zeal for His Father's house, with zeal for truth and justice, yet patient and pitiful even as He smites, gentle as the gentlest mother.

9. All this we see and much more; the love of loneliness, though "his delights are to be with the children of men"; the love of prayer, though He cannot tear Himself from the crowd, not even to take food; the love of peace, though His days are one long warfare; the love, seen in His very outward behavior to be one with all men, though He could not keep from them that which prompted them to make Him their king. But it is useless to carry on the portrayal; we go on and on, the fascination grows, at each new step we see more and more, for He is utterly transparent; and yet at every point at which we stop we feel that we have said nothing. The Evangelists knew better than we, and they did not venture to describe Him. They were content to let Him walk through their narrative, preaching the Kingdom, healing the sick, having compassion on the multitude, or retiring into the mountain to pray, knowing well that in so doing He would not be lost amid the details; His personality would be too great for that; they knew they would, in their simple story of simple fact, leave behind them that on which all generations would ponder, yet which they would never exhaust.

10. And indeed it is so. The more we contemplate it, look at it with believing eyes, warmed by love, stirred by hope and trust, the more vivid does the portrait grow, the more living are the features. They exist, we know them; "we have found him whom our soul loveth, we have held him and will not let him go." Other portraits help, copies, facsimiles, drawn by more recent artists; but all these have their limitations, some have their exaggerations, none are exactly accurate; all have what life they possess from the great original, and only in so far as they reproduce its fire have they any inspiration in themselves.

—excerpted from *A More Excellent Way*
by Alban Goodier, S.J.
Courtesy Grail Publications

9

FINDING JESUS THROUGH INCIDENTS IN JOHN AND TEACHINGS IN MATTHEW

I. How to Meditate on Incidents in the Life of Jesus. *From St. John.*

Meditations. Some suggestions:

1. *Use your imagination.* In your mind, go to the scene. What is the country like? The local setting?

Then 1) Look carefully at who is there—the kinds of people, the expressions on their faces.

2) Listen to what they are saying and in what tones of voice, with what feeling.

3) Attend to what they are doing. What's it like to be there?

From this try to gain some lesson;
Profit and talk with the Lord as moved.

Try this on—

The Call of the Apostles John 1:35-50

2. Take the part of one of the persons in the scene.

Try to imagine as well as you can—even in smallest details—what he is thinking, feeling and doing, as he moves through the scene or event. How does he look at it all? Try to understand and feel for him—even talk with him about it with him if you like. You may love, grieve, be glad—as you feel moved.

Try this on—

> *The Wedding at Cana* John 2:1-11

Alternative: As reverently and completely as you can, take the part of Jesus: What is *He* thinking, feeling, doing as He moves through each part of this scene?

---

3. Ask Questions (as in Meeting 8)

e.g. Which person are you in this scene? Why?

What is so important about this event: Where does this fit into all Jesus came to accomplish?

Is there anything about Jesus here which captivates you, or draws you to love Him?

Is there any way He would like you to carry on the work you see Him doing here?

Is there anything here which tells you how you could be more like Him in the way you look at life or people— or try to cope with either?

What has this to do with the Church or society; my family or neighbors?

Who, What, Why, Where, When, How, For Whom, and Does it all Make any Difference?

Try this on—

> *Cleansing of the Temple* John 2:13-17 or
> *Multiplication of the Loaves* John 6:1-15

---

4. "Be there" in your imagination. This time, be a bystander. Mentally rest in

the scene. Make no special effort to do anything but "be there." Simply watch, listen, and let it all work on you—let it suggest such thoughts and feelings as may come. Just stay and watch.

Try this on—
> *Walking on the Sea* John 6:16-21
> (If you were going to describe your reactions to a friend, what would you say?)

---

5. **Goodier.** Meditate on the selection from Archbishop Goodier (on the separate sheet) or on a selection from another author. Notice the warmth and attraction he finds in Christ. Reflect about how to get an interior "feel" for Jesus such as he seems to have had.

II. **How to Meditate on Jesus' Teachings.** *From St. Matthew.*

To meditate on teachings or "sermon-like" material:

Read the text three times. Pause after each reading:
  after the first to recall: What did Jesus say?
      (Were you concentrating?)
  after the second to "listen," then to think: What does this mean?
      Why did Jesus say or do it, etc.? (See Questions in Meeting 8, if you wish.)
  after the third to pray—speaking directly with Jesus, the Father
      or some person in the scene.

Meditations:
  6. Matthew 5:1-12 The Beatitudes
  7. Matthew 5:13-16 Salt of the Earth; Light of the World
  8. Matthew 6:1-6 Almsgiving in secret; Prayer in secret

9. Matthew 6:25-34 Trust in Providence
10. Matthew 7:3-5 Do not judge.

—Text for Practice Meditation—

John 1:35-36.

> The next day John was there again with two of his disciples. As he watched Jesus walk by he said, "Look! There is the Lamb of God." The two disciples heard what he said, and followed Jesus.

Notice how rewriting this passage into sense lines brings out meanings:

> The next day—
> John was there again
> with two of his disciples.
> As he watched Jesus walk by,
> he said, "Look!
> There is the Lamb of God."
> The two disciples heard what he said,
> and followed Jesus.

Try rewriting passages in this way.
With a little practice you will find you can
meditate over almost any clause or phrase.

—A Brief Summary of Meditation Helps—

Preliminaries:
1. Relax. Breathe. Recall His presence.
2. Skim the passage. Visualize the scene.
3. Ask for some definitive grace or profit.

Meditation:
4. Read passage slowly. Let yourself become aware of interior attraction.
5. Linger over what seems fruitful.
6. If nothing does, reread, more slowly, and ask questions, or use your imagination, or just sit quietly before it again for awhile.
7. Pause at any time for conversation with the Lord—especially at the conclusion of your meditation.

A More Excellent Way (cont.)

This is some little shadow of Jesus as the Gospels show Him to us; more if we like, and, above all, more of the details, we can gather for ourselves. These are four guiding lines; we can easily cluster much else around them. For He is not difficult to discover; He needs no great effort of psychology or analysis: He is Himself just simple and true, just meek and humble of heart, and by truth and simplicity, by humility and meekness, He is best to be found. Let us not forget His own prayer of thanksgiving wrung from Him at a moment when the learned turned away in scorn: "Heavenly Father, I give thee thanks that thou has hidden these things from the wise and prudent, and hast revealed them to little ones." Nor again His other words of warning: "Unless you become as little children, you shall not enter into the Kingdom of God."

It is worth our while to weigh the meaning of these words. We complain of our want of fruit in prayer; of its dryness, its emptiness; often we only mean, but we do not know it, that we are looking for fruit, not of prayer, but of study; we are watching for that reflex knowledge that comes of thought and study, not for that deeper insight, that fuller understanding, that realization which is found in faith and love and hope, which is the real fruit of prayer, and which can no more be weighed and measured than life itself can be weighed in pounds or measured by yards. In other words, we judge by the standards of poor grown-up people, and not by the unerring standard of a child. A child needs but its mother's company to know her, to love her, to trust her, yet its knowledge, and love, and trust are not less true, or less complete, or less admirable on that account. And in precisely the same way there is a knowledge of Our Lord which no books or pondering can give us; which can be gained only by living in His company; by living in His company as He glides through the pages of the Gospels; as he plies His daily trade at Nazareth, quiet, monotonous, till we become almost forgetful of His presence; or creeps away in silence up the mountain-side, till that too, becomes a habit with us; or walks by the riverside, unnoticed in the crowd, except by one who alone has eyes to see—how strange that those who fail to see Him claim this as proof of their superior knowledge! —or stands firm and frank before the people, now appealing, now commanding, now consoling, now rebuking, but always the same strong pillar on which all may lean; or sits at table, now with friends, now with enemies, familiarly treated, yet always reverenced, condemned by some, yet feared by others, held in awe, yet never losing that which is expressed in the phrase "only Jesus"; or sleeps in the boat, feeble, yet almighty; or compassionates by lowering Himself to the lowest, yet in such a way that because of it men would hail Him as their King; or denounces evil with a thunder that cows the most violent, yet all the while infants clamber on His knee—living with Him in the midst of all this, in busy streets or along lonely byways, in public Jerusalem or in the privacy of Bethany, we come to know Him as He is for ourselves, and we know that we know Him, whatever those who know Him not may say, and even though we have not, nor care to have a single word with which to express it. "It is the Lord!" "I to my beloved and my beloved to me." "I know in whom I have believed." That is enough.

My Lord Jesus Christ, Thou Wonder of the world, most beautiful among the sons of men, before whom Thy very enemies bow down, acknowledging the marvel of Thy countenance, the perfection of Thy character, the invincible attraction of Thy whole self, how strange a thing it is that there can be those who pass Thee by unnoticed, how stranger still that even we pass Thee by! Yet is it even so. We believe, we are certain, we know; we build our life here, and our hope hereafter, on Thee and Thy claim; we own Thee; not only to be perfect Man, but to be very God of very God; we see in Thee alpha and omega, the beginning and the end, the climax of all for which this world was made, the source from which flows whatever of good this world contains; we can see all this, and know it to be true, and in our moments of emotion can think we would gladly give our lives to witness to its truth; and yet the next minute we can ignore Thee; we can go counter to Thee; we can go our way through life as if Thou hadst never been.

More than this. We who have the light can reach behind the simple story of the Gospels; with Thy Apostle St. Paul to guide us we can understand in part what Thy Resurrection signified; that "having once risen thou diest now no more, death can no more have dominion over thee"; that therefore Thou art living now as Thou wast living then, the same Jesus now as then, the same utter truth, the same fascination, the same understanding sympathy, the same beating heart: "Jesus Christ yesterday, today and the same for ever." We can realize all this, understand it sufficiently to know that it is true; we can accept the fact of Thy being, and of Thy nearness to us here and now; and yet we can think, and act, and build up our lives as if it were not or as if to us it meant nothing. We can, with eyes of faith, see Thy face glowing in the darkness; with consciousness of hope we can feel thy hands stretched out to seize our own; with the instinct of love we can distinguish the very accent of Thy voice; even as did thy fellow-country-men of Galilee, calling to us, whispering our very names, telling us of love that human words cannot express—all this is ours, and by its very clearness we know it to be true; it is no fancy, it is the offshoot of no mere sentiment; and yet withal we can turn away, our vision obscured by the fascination of a trifle; and we can act as if we had never learnt to "taste and see how sweet is the Lord!"

Nay, there is something more. We can hear Thee, in words that true hearing cannot misunderstand, giving Thyself to us to be our slave, to be our food, our life, our abiding companion; yet we can still remain unmoved. One or two among men in the ages past we can see who have learnt Thee, and, once they have learnt, have counted all else but refuse in comparison; who have loved Thee, and once they have begun to love, have known for certain that no other love could draw them away, with this no other love could compare; who have given themselves to Thee, and once they have made the surrender, have then proved what heroism, what a true man's strength can accomplish—the strength that conquers torture, that makes a toy of death; the strength that magically turns everything to gladness. We can all see this; we can admire and approve; we can say that here is a man at his best, because he has found the true goal of his being, has attained to that likeness to Jesus which is man's ideal—all this we can see, and can say, and then can turn about upon our heel and go our way, as if for us these things had no meaning.

Truly, what a strange thing is man! Whether it be the man who believes, yet is not subdued, or the man who will not believe, as if to believe so grand and great a truth were in some way demeaning to himself. Demeaning to acknowledge Jesus Christ! Demeaning to own Him for my Brother, whose kinship makes me royal! To call Him my friend, whose great heart expands mine beyond the limits of the world! To take Him for my companion, whose comradeship gives life a new meaning! To accept Him for my Leader, whose service is a hall-mark of nobility! To set Him up for my Ideal man which neither God nor man could make anything more grand! Demeaning to be won by Jesus Christ! If man thinks so, or if in his meanness he acts so, can he be worth so great a gift? Can he be worth the offering of the life, the outpouring of the blood, of Jesus?

Yes; even to this Christ says, "Yes"; and it is a last disclosure of His character, the crowning feature of all, a revelation, which breaks down the heart of St. Paul, and would break down the heart of every man who would let himself be penetrated by it. "Christ loved me, even me, and gave himself, for me, even for me."

When I was younger, a novice in religion, and knew myself less, and knew others less, and was full of high ambitions in the spiritual life, and sought in books and in study, in thought-out plans and schemes on paper for guides to the summit of perfection I set virtues before me, and meditated on their beauty, and proposed to myself to acquire them, sub-dividing them, analyzing them, arranging their degrees as the steps of a ladder. This week, as the good spiritual writers bade me, I would acquire the virtue of patience; next week it should be a carefully guarded tongue; the week after should be given to charity; then should come the spirit of prayer; and in a month or two, perhaps, I might have an ecstasy and "see the Lord." But now, when I have grown older, and find myself still struggling for the first of these virtues, and that in a very elementary degree, and have been taught quite other lessons than I dreamt of, in part by the sorry disappointments in my own soul, in part by the progress seen in the souls of others, I am convinced that there is one road to perfection better than all else—in fact, that if we neglect this one no other will be of much avail. After all, it is possible to acquire perfection in virtues, and yet to be far from a saint; few men have made better use of the particular examination of conscience, for the acquiring of natural virtues, than a certain well-known atheist, and yet to the end he remained without a spark of religion in him. On the other hand, it is possible to be a great saint, and yet to be imperfect in many respects; ask the saints themselves and they will all tell you of their many failures and shortcomings. But one thing is not possible; it is not possible to grow in the knowledge, and love, and imitation of Jesus Christ, without at the same time growing in the perfection of every virtue and becoming more a saint every day.

This, then, if I were allowed to begin my spiritual life over again, is the line along which I would try to live it; and is the line along which I would try to lead the lives of any whom God gave into my care. Particular virtues are good things—of course they are; it is much to be always patient, to be diligent in the use of our time, to be considerate with those who try us, to keep our tongue in control; nevertheless, "Do not the heathens this?" And is it not possible to possess all these, and yet, on their very account, to remain as proud as Lucifer? I would go further and say that the devil himself must possess many of these virtues; he can certainly bide his time, he can be very busy, he can speak honeyed words, he can accommodate himself to everybody's needs, he can be the most attractive of companions. But these things are not the main issue; they are often no more than the paint on the surface; and true sanctity only begins when the core of the creature is affected. And this is done, almost alone, by love; when the creature loves, then it is changed, and till then scarcely at all. Thus it is that the knowledge and love of Jesus Christ goes deeper down than any Stoic striving after virtue; it is flesh and blood where the other is but bleached bones; it gives life and substance where the other is only dead perfection; the imitation of Jesus Christ includes every virtue, makes them unconsciously our own, produces them from itself, and does not merely put them on from without, even as the brown earth gives for the beauty of spring flowers and does not know it.

—*Alban Goodier, S.J.*

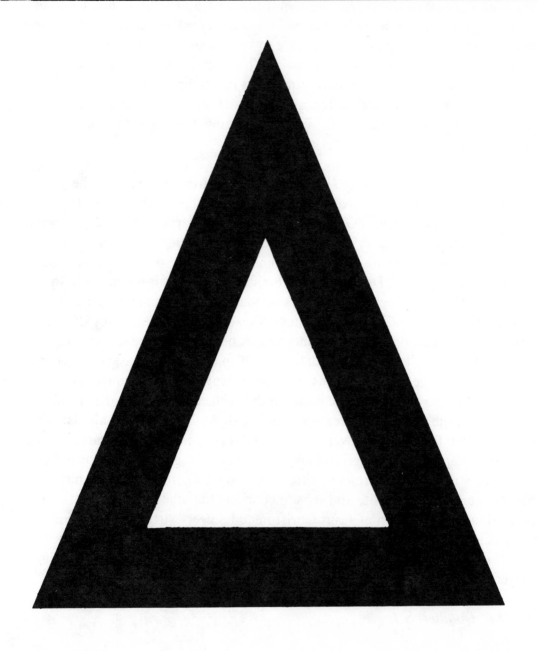

10

FINDING JESUS THROUGH LUKE, "THE SCRIBE OF THE MEEKNESS OF CHRIST"

"We have saved the best wine until last. . . ."
Luke's portrait of Jesus is the most humanly appealing.

Directions:

Read the Scripture passage. To pray, allow it to affect you. Give yourself some time in quiet to react. Then if needed, use one or two of the Thought Questions.

Address the Question directly to Jesus or the Father if you like.

In due time, let your reactions or reflections lead to some response: to wonder, love, sense of one's littleness, some resolve, further questions, etc.

And conclude every meditation by talking intimately for a short time with Jesus.

To foster intimacy with Jesus in prayer (to get to know Him for oneself, find Him, feel closer to Him):

   a) pause frequently to listen or to converse briefly—especially at the close. (Use your own words. Share feelings.)

   b) recall how much you love or admire a husband or wife, dear friend or associate, and try somehow to transfer that same kind of feeling to Christ.

   c) as you look at the scene try to become more aware that He is still that very same person today—the same you meet in the Eucharist, call on in need, etc.

   d) look for everything in the passage which attracts you,—for example, how Godlike He is, yet how human, how compassionate, yet how strong.

Meditations:

1. 4:40-44   Various Miracles
2. 5:27-32   Call of Levi
3. 7:36-50   Penitent Woman
4. 9:57-62   Conditions of Discipleship (see also 14:25-35)
5. 10:29-37   Good Samaritan
6. 11:1-13   Prayer
7. 14:12-24   The Poor
8. 15:1-7   Lost Sheep; or 15:11-32 Prodigal Son
9. 18:15-17   Jesus Blesses Children
10. 19:11-26 Accountability for Talents

Remember your aim in prayer:
    to see Thee more clearly,
    love Thee more dearly,
    and follow Thee more nearly—
    in that special way that is yours.

THOUGHT QUESTIONS—STARTERS FOR PRAYER

*(Try one; and address Questions directly to Jesus
at any time in your prayer if you wish)*

1) What response was Jesus seeking immediately? In the long run?
(Dear Lord, what result—why did you do or say this? What was it you
wanted to happen? Did it? Were you happy about the reaction . . .?)

2) What does or could this symbolize?
(Dear Lord, are you somehow telling me or us more than meets the eye?
Why are you saying it this way—I wonder if I were in your situation how
I would have tried to put the message . . .?)

3) Is there something here of comfort? Is there Light in the Darkness?
(Dear Lord, When you said or did this, did you have any idea how many
people would read or hear about it? Did you intend somehow to make

their lives, or our lives, more livable? Are you somehow saying, in the struggle, "Be of good heart?" Or is that why you inspired St. Luke to write it—I wonder if I couldn't draw on it . . .?)

4) Is there something here for me?

(Dear Lord, does what you said or did tell me anything about the special and unique way you are calling me to follow you as one of my age, and all the rest that make me *me*?)

Others:

5) Daily Life. Has the passage implications for eating, drinking, sleeping, talking, working, raising the family . . . the things in which most people spend most of their time?

6) Jesus. What does the passage tell you about Jesus, the way He looks at life or people, the way He makes His choice? What is the obvious message? What the deeper implications? (What does it show about His mission, His attitudes or values, or who He is?)

7) The Human Condition. Has the passage—what Jesus said or did— any implications for the hopes and dreams in the heart of each person?

8) The Transcendent God. Is there something here of mystery, revelation—something more than meets the eye? (Almost a call to worship?)

9) The Message. Is there something here that all the world should know about? (Who will tell them? Will anyone listen?)

10) Centering Within. Look deep within yourself . . . . as deeply as you possibly can. Does or could this passage touch anything at the deepest level of your heart or being? Is it calling, confronting, disturbing, alluring, somehow touching you at the core or center of all that is you? Is it asking for radical change?

11) Our Times. Could what Jesus said or did apply to our times. How so?

E.g. To a current social problem?
      To conflicts between nations? Or those in our own?

To contemporary standards in morals, living or art?
To social concerns of the Church? Or in our community?
To how to live, love, grow, choose or be happy?
To our notions of beauty or success?
To the pace at which we live; or the comfort; or poverty?
To problems of authority?
To conflict in the world of work?
To our notion of religion, culture, nationhood or Church?
To our hopes and our dreams?
To the creativity of man?
To the meaning of life?

12) The Long View. What has this incident to do with the history of Jesus' life? With the history of man? With my personal history—the growth stages in my becoming? To what does it point for the future?

"MARANATHA"—COME LORD JESUS

TEXTS FOR PRACTICE

Luke 4:40-44

At sunset, all who had people sick with a variety of diseases took them to him, and He laid hands on each of them and cured them. Demons departed from many, crying out as they did so, "You are the Son of God!" He rebuked them and did not allow them to speak because they knew he was the Messiah.

The next morning, He left the town and set out into the open country. The crowds went in search of him, and when they found him, they tried to keep him from leaving them. But He said to them, "To other towns I must announce the good news of the reign of God, because that is why I was sent." And he continued to preach in the synagogues of Judea.

Luke 5:27-32

Afterwards, He went out and saw a tax collector named Levi sitting at his customs post. He said to him "Follow Me." Leaving everything behind, he stood up and became his follower. After that, Levi gave a great reception for Jesus in his house, in which he was joined by a large crowd of tax-collectors and others at dinner. The Pharisees and Scribes of their party said to his disciples, "Why do you eat and drink with the tax-collectors and non-observers of the law?" Jesus said to them, "The healthy do not need a doctor, sick people do. I have not come to invite the self-righteous to a change of heart, but sinners."

INTRODUCTION TO SCRIPTURE

Scripture scholars these days are paying a lot more attention to how history was written at the time the Gospels were written. They find that history then was often written more like a play, a collection of sayings, a historical novel— rather than straight reporting. Events—things that really happened—were often adorned somewhat artificially with details to bring out their meaning. The author had no TV or newspaper to check out the details—and since the point lay in the significance and meaning of the event itself—the details may have been imagined to help make his point.

Religious history was written the same way. This may seem not quite proper by our standards for writing history; nevertheless, this was the accepted way to write about God's action in history at that time—so no one challenged it. Thus not all details in Scripture are exact, for the simple reason that the author never intended them as such.

Then can one still rely on the Bible? One certainly can—events are there, but accuracy of details shouldn't be pushed. However, for practical purposes of this course, you may take whatever message from the text you can pray over. That will serve for prayer.

To really get into this question—about historical accuracy—would be a course in itself. But it isn't necessary for a prayer course. What is necessary for prayer is that you open your hearts so that the Holy Spirit may speak to you through his word—His inspired word—so that He may help you find meaning in it for your life and may help you to more intimate contact with Jesus in prayer. For this you need only the inspired text. It was inspired precisely as written.

A good short introduction to such questions may be found in the introductions or forewords to some Bibles. Read these. Most people ignore them. Thus the twenty-five or so pages which open the St. Joseph Edition of the New American Bible—our ordinary Catholic version—will provide a good start, and an eye-opener to those for whom this is new ground. We urge it to the reading of all, but strongly repeat that concern for such questions be not allowed to get in the way of praying over Scripture as Christians have been doing for hundreds of years—with or without the benefit of the new scholarship. Let such concerns not get in the way of a more intimate relationship with the Lord, nor your perceiving from this course a fuller overview of what it means to be a Christian: a follower of Jesus in the work of His Kingdom.

11

FOLLOWING JESUS IN HIS LOVE FOR EACH PERSON

*Meetings 11-15 invite our trying to follow more closely—
and become a little more like—Jesus.*

Three Meditations: The *Why* of love: Why we must manage, somehow, to love *everyone.*

1. I am one with Jesus.

Read Acts of the Apostles 9:1-5: Paul is called by Jesus. In Verses 4-5: "Saul, why do you persecute Me . . .," Jesus identifies Himself with us! This is one of the most important insights in all of Scripture. Let yourself sense—almost feel, if you can, the deep level of oneness that exists between your own self and Christ. Try to get deeply impressed with this fact. What does it mean for practical life?

2. We are all one in the Lord.

Read 1 Corinthians 12:12-27: In this reading Paul theologizes that Christ forms one body with us. We are one in the Lord! What are the most important consequences you can think of to this amazing fact? Let yourself try to sense—to almost feel—your oneness-in-Christ with some person, or some group, in your life. Like limbs or branches we share a common life.

3. Since this is so . . .

Read Romans 12:3-21. More theologizing plus applications to a life of practical Christian love. What has been your own history of interpersonal relationships? Do you get along with people better than you used to? Are there any with whom you don't? How can one love everyone?

Seven Meditations: The Art of Loving.

Directions:
The next seven meditations constitute a mini-course in the art of Christian loving: three meditations about loving; evaluate; then three more.

Each meditation should be made as follows: Read the text. Ask the Lord to help you know and plan what to do about it in some one particular situation. Be very specific: To whom? Where? When? How?

Picture yourself actually doing exactly what you plan—talking, acting and feeling the way you want to, using the facial expression, tone of voice, etc. Be very detailed about this. Have you some model?

Repeat the imagery, *and the feeling you want to accompany it*, several times to deepen the impression.

Leave—try to leave—the meditation "rarin to go," eager to try it in practice. Again, ask His help.

Note: For best results it is recommended that this visualization be repeated for fifteen or so minutes each day for two to three weeks. Positive emotional tone, such as a feeling of pleasure or satisfaction, should accompany the imagery.

---

4. Love Appreciates and is Thankful.

Today: Encourage or praise. Give recognition or support to several persons. Give thanks—to wife, friends, store-clerk, fellow-workers. A word of praise or encouragement keeps many a person or enterprise operating at a higher and sometimes more Christian level. "I can live for two months on a good compliment."

—*Mark Twain*

5. Love is Compassionate—Understands—Doesn't Judge—Listens

Pick any of the following:

a) *Compassionate*—

Today: Try to feel compassion. How many persons right before your eyes are ill, in prison, in some sort of need . . . . (everything in Matthew 25:31-46). They are not always easy to relate to. But they probably cope with life as best they can. (Don't we all?)

b) *Understands*—

Today: Try understanding each person you meet, or one particular person—understanding how they look at things—from their point of view. They may have some secret cross—perhaps a temperament quite different from yours and more difficult to manage. They may be handling themselves better than they seem. Try deliberately to put yourself in their shoes.

c) *Doesn't Judge*—

Today: Don't judge anyone. No criticism or negative remarks about anyone. Not even politicians! (Feel sorry for them if you like!) And distance yourself from coldness or criticism you yourself may receive . . . . (because)

"They may be having a bad day—in fact, they've been having a lot of them lately!" Remember that human crudeness, aloofness, and anger are often really cries of hurt.

d) *Listens*—

Today: Listen to each person. Say very little—just listen. Listen especially to the tone of voice in which they speak—the emotional tone beneath their words. What are they feeling, as revealed in how they speak? Try to respond to that tone, if you can.

6. Love Shows in Action.

A day of courtesies, a smile, some warmth. Pleasant speech—a few good turns—or a few phone calls to encourage, approve, or just lighten the burden!

7. Day for Evaluation.

Reflect on the *Thoughts* on pp. 90-91.

Then re-read the directions for meditating (above) and consider: Did you really follow them? How well did the meditations work? For the next three days should you repeat 4-5-6, follow with 8-9-10, or design your own?

8. Love Begins Where You Are

Read 1 Corinthians 13:1-8. How does it apply to your life? What are your possibilities for *growing in love precisely* because you are what you are— precisely and just especially because you are young or old, black or white, handsome or average, sick or well, with such or such a cross, with this or that talent?

your topic: your role or position *precisely as* single, married, black, white, successful or not, young, middleaged or old, having a certain appearance, temperament, or condition of health.

9. Patience . . . ! Calm . . . !

Read Ephesians 4:26-32 and/or Colossians 3:12-17
Reflect: Some periods of the day, and some persons . . . can be exceptionally trying.

88

Pick out one or the other and visualize some alternatives for bettering the situation or healing the relationship. Ask help, light and grace.

---

10. Love is Faithful

In an age when so many seem to accept the practice of ripping off, and are sometimes unfaithful to promises, how can we Christians bring more of trust, faithfulness, and integrity into relationships with one another and into the fabric of our society?
See 1 Corinthians 1:9

An Alternate Topic: Reflect on *Friendship.* See Sirach (Ecclesiasticus) 6:5-17

> Christ has no body on earth but yours,
> no hands on earth but your hands.
> Yours are the eyes through which He
> looks out with compassion
> upon the world.
> Yours the feel with which He
> chooses to go about doing good.
> For as He is the head,
> so we are the members.

Community: *Two Texts*

Acts 2:42-47

They devoted themselves to the apostles' instruction and the communal life, to the breaking of bread and the prayers. A reverent fear overtook them all, for many wonders and signs were performed by the apostles. Those who believed shared all things in common; they would sell their property and goods dividing everything on the basis of each one's needs. They went to the temple area every day, while in their homes they broke bread. With exultant and sincere hearts they took their meals in common, praising God and winning the approval of all the people. Day by day the Lord added to their number those who were being saved.

Acts 4:32-35

The community of believers were of one heart and one mind. None of them even claimed anything as his own; rather, everything was held in common. With power the apostles bore witness to the resurrection of the Lord Jesus, and great respect was paid to them all; nor was there anyone needy among them, for all who owned property or houses sold them and donated the proceeds. They used to lay them at the feet of the apostles to be distributed to everyone according to his need.

THOUGHTS

Oh Lord,
today let my words be tender and sweet,
for tomorrow I may have to eat them.
—*Source unknown*

As the cow said to the Maine farmer,
"Thank you for a warm hand on a cold morning."
—*The Kennedy Wit*

There is something wrong with a man
as there is with a motor
   when he knocks continually.
—*Source unknown*

I have never thought much of the courage of the lion-tamer,
Inside the cage, he is at least safe from other men.
—*George Bernard Shaw*

Christian love is "anyhow" love.

It means I love you anyhow—whether you're white, black, green, or purple, up, down, good, bad, nice, ornery, and above all whether you accept me, reject me, ignore me or hate me. . . .

I love you anyhow. (*Jesus did!*)

(Jesus, waiting for someone, asks)

"Is that Thomas back?"
"No Lord, it is a group of students."
"And?"
"They've signed a petition."
It says they love you
no matter whose son you are.
They love your gentleness,
tolerance and humility.
They want you to know, that they
don't care if you're God or not. . . ." (!)
—*A.J. Langguth*

Is something keeping you from Christian love—for everyone? Fear of being hurt or rejected? Not enough true love for self?

"I never met a man I didn't like."
—*Will Rogers*

As often as you did it for one of my least brothers, you did it for me.
—*Jesus*

12

FOLLOWING JESUS IN HIS LOVE FOR ALL MEN

Meditations.

1. **Planning Your Prayer for the Next Two Weeks** (*in case you want review or change of pace.*)

Some possibilities:
   a) Review former meditations.
   b) Read a commentary on a Gospel. Or read Introductory Notes to a Bible.
   c) Talk with others about something that has to do with Religion or prayer.
   d) Proceed with topics about "Following Jesus in His Love For All Men" (as below)
   e) Rest. Do your own thing. Eastern Prayer? Visit a Prayer Group?
   f) Spend two more weeks working on personal relationships.
   g) Consider your worst problem and how to manage it better.
   h) Consider your prayer style. Experiment.
   i) Each day, read a story, or newspaper article, see a movie, or watch TV program and meditate on it.
   j) Do Whatever you think would bring you closer to Jesus, His Spirit or the Father.

2-10: Introduction:

If you decide to proceed to new meditations, use those below. They invite us to reach in love to all the world as Jesus did. Meditations 2-6 invite reaching out directly; 7-10, indirectly.

2. Concern for Current Problems: Summary of *Octogesima Adveniens*— (*Apostolic Letter of Pope Paul VI, May, 1971.*)

Paul said the Christian must assume a political and social obligation in the society in which he lives to combat the evils he finds. He said Christians must be concerned with:

Problems of urbanization and crowded suburbs;
Social, religious, and political discrimination;
Crime waves, eroticism, and the use of drugs;
The ferment of youth;
The emancipation of women and the rights of workers;
The need of tackling new problems with bright new ideas.

In His days, was Jesus concerned with such problems?
Is He—does He want us to be—concerned with them today? To what degree?
In our day, what is the best way to "follow Jesus in His love for all men?"

---

3. Concern for Social Order: Quotation from *Pacem in Terris* (Peace on Earth) —Encyclical Letter of Pope John XXIII, April, 1963, #146, 147

"Once again, we deem it opportune to remind our children of their duty to take an active part in public life and to contribute toward the attainment of the common good of the entire human family as well as to that of their own political community. They should endeavor, therefore, in the light of their Christian faith and led by love, to insure that the various institutions —whether economic, social, cultural or political in purpose—should be such as . . . . to facilitate or render less arduous man's perfecting of himself in both the natural order and the supernatural.

"Again . . . . in order to imbue civilization with sound principles and enliven it with the spirit of the gospel, it is not enough to be illumined with the gift of faith and enkindled with the desire of forwarding a good cause;

it is also necessary to take an active part in the various organizations and influence them from within. . . ."

Read and think about this quotation slowly—one phrase at a time. (Almost any phrase could make a meditation! For example, how shall we "imbue civilization with sound principles?")

---

4. Communicate.

Plan to write or phone some individual person in order to approve or object to something, or to encourage or comfort.

Pray over your plan as you did last time; visualize in detail, and feel glad about what you intend to do. You may pray for such gladness. Conclude by reflecting on Colossians 4:3-6.

---

5. Study.

Read Meditations (2) and (3) again. Then plan to study further, read an article or engage someone in conversation about a topic mentioned in (2) or (3) (a social concern of the Church). Pray as above; and pray for some useful insight, or profit from the study or conversation.

---

6. Act.

Read James 2:14-17 and consider: Christ needs action in homes and places of business. Would it be possible for you to influence one or the other toward functioning in a more fully Christian way? Pray as above and ask for some profit from your prayer and effort.

7. Everyone Is Important

The key to world-wide influence for everyone from day-to-day living, even if ill or elderly, is found in *The Mystical Body* Encyclical (*Mystici Corporis*) by Pope Pius XII, 1943. Read the following quotation prayerfully and thoughtfully. It is a profound statement. The Encyclical tells us that Christ not only wants our help to save and redeem the world —He actually needs it! He has decided to make our help and partnership with Himself absolutely indispensable for the saving of all men. Here is how Pius II explains it:

#55 "Moreover . . . . in carrying out the work of redemption He (Christ) wishes to be helped by the members of His Body. This is not because He is indigent and weak but rather because He has so willed it for the greater glory of His unspotted Spouse (the Church). Dying on the cross, He left to His Church the immense treasury of the redemption; toward this she contributed nothing. But when these graces come to be distributed, not only does He share this task of sanctification with His Church, but He wants it in a way to be due to her action.

Deep mystery this, subject of inexhaustible meditation: that the salvation of many depends on the prayers and voluntary penances which the members of the Mystical Body of Jesus Christ offer for this intention, and on the assistance . . . . of the faithful, especially fathers and mothers of families, which they must offer to their divine saviour as though they were His associates."

#125-126-127 For though our Saviour's cruel passion and death merited for His Church an infinite treasure of graces, God's inscrutable providence has decreed that these abundant graces should not be granted all at once; and the amount of grace to be given depends in no small part also on our good deeds . . . . These heavenly gifts will surely flow more abundantly if we . . . . pray . . . . especially if by participating, even

daily if possible, in the Eucharistic Sacrifice . . and finally humbly accept from God's hands the burdens and sorrows of this present life. Thus, according to the apostle, 'we shall fill up those things that are wanting of the sufferings of Christ, in our flesh, for his body, which is the Church'. . . . Let them remember that their sufferings are not in vain, but they will be to their great gain and that of the Church, if for this purpose they but take courage and bear them with patience.

To those who want to do more for the Kingdom but feel hindered by age, health, or circumstances, these texts should be highly consoling. They tell us we can!

> For this meditation: Re-read and fix the thoughts of the above quotation deeply in your memory. Meditations 8-9-10 will offer suggestions for putting them to practice in everyday living.

---

8. Suffering.

In the spirit of love—following the Lord in love for all men—plan to suffer an anxiety, bodily ailment, or circumstantial trial with an entirely new spirit and outlook: for some world or community need. No day in which you have so suffered is useless! In your meditation, plan and visualize how you'll carry that next cross. Repeat the visualization several times. (Ask the Lord to help you remember your plan when the time comes . . . .)

---

9. Offering: Prayer and Duty

Re-read the first part of the Encyclical text (#55).
Then plan to offer some prayer, or duty-done-well for a world or community need. Any day with such prayer or work offered—is a good day.

The beauty and efficacy of offering routine tasks, performed well and lovingly, for the benefit of the Kingdom should be stressed. It is highly practical, accomplishes great good and is within the reach of all. It's worth the admonition: Think about it—and do something.

Conclude with Colossians 3:17.

---

10. Penance.

Re-read the second part of the Encyclical text (#125, 126, 127) *and* Colossians 1:24.

Then plan to perform an act of penance, small or large—preferably small, but to be done with a great deal of love. Love matters; intention matters. Any day in which you have deliberately done penance for a worthwhile cause is a worthwhile day. Remember that the same is true of involuntary suffering and anxiety accepted and borne in the same spirit. That is an important point. So many of us waste our crosses. If we could only remember to do with ours what Jesus did with His! Pray for this grace.

Synopsis of PRAY

God and Me.

    1. Communicating with God—and—Loving Yourself
    2. Life has a Meaning.
    3. Everything Has a Purpose.
    4. Obstacles to Love: Sin and Self-Centeredness. "Repent . . ."
    5. Pause to Refresh.

The Kingdom.

    6. The Good News: The Kingdom is Here.
    7. Preparing for Jesus (Christmas): I. Advent Prayer
                                        II. Religion in the Home.

—CHRISTMAS—

Finding Jesus

   8. Finding (getting to know) Jesus Through the Gospel of Mark

   9. Finding Jesus Through Incidents in John and Teachings in Matthew.

  10. Finding Jesus Through Luke, "The Scribe of the Meekness of Christ."

Following Jesus.

  11. Following Jesus in His Love for Each Individual

  12. Following Jesus in His Love for All Men

  13. Following Jesus Through Luke, "The Scribe of the Meekness of Christ."

—EASTER—

Better Prayer.

  14. Better Prayer Amid The Hustle and Bustle

  15. The Holy Spirit—and—Planning for Growth.

MEETING
13

FOLLOWING JESUS THROUGH A PERSONAL COMMITMENT
ALSO: THE MASS AS A CALL TO COMMITMENT

1. Following Jesus by a Commitment-to-Praying. *Is it for me?*

Reflect:

A commitment is a love-pledge to another person. This course could easily issue in one of two commitments to Jesus. The first is to prayer.

Consider whether somehow, for the rest of your life, you desire that no day shall pass without prayer contact with your Beloved, even be it only a silent, tired resting in His presence at the end of the day. If not daily, then at least with that frequency which nourishes friendship—which makes room for Him in your life. This is what is meant by a commitment to Praying.

You say you love God and wish Him to be First in your life? Then spend time together. How many husbands say to their wives: "You know, I love you. I give you everything. I work day and night for you." But she replies, "But you never *tell* me you do." Does *He* deserve any less than similar attention? The How and the When is what is being proposed for your consideration.

Living for the love and service of others is highly to be praised. The same for liturgical and formal prayers. But neither of these is precisely designed for that special personal intimacy with the Lord known only in private prayer which shares kinship with that sweet interchange, that holding of hands and hearts, bodies and souls, known to lovers.

Is such a commitment for me?

2. Following Jesus by a Deeper—More Total Commitment: *Is it for me?*

A second commitment for your consideration is more radical. It involves trying to turn ourselves over to Him with that faith and trust He kept asking of His followers. Ordinarily, this means within the vocation, occupation and state of life we have already chosen. And sometimes, instead of some radical change, what it may mean most of all is simply opening oneself entirely to taking oneself and one's life *as it is*, and resolving to make the most of it rather than sorrowing and pining for what cannot be. But it's much deeper than commitment to Sunday Mass, trying to lead a good life and being helpful to others—though it will show itself by these.

It is the invitation to become more completely a disciple, to make a more complete gift of oneself to Jesus. It is the invitation to make Him the center of one's life, as did the early Christians. It is the invitation to take the "leap of faith" in trying to accept Him and all He stands for as prior to all other considerations in life. It is trying to acknowledge Him as Lord in such a way that He and His pleasure motivate our choices.

This "Yes" may be the result of slow growth or sudden insight. It is the full, conscious, mature-adult response to the invitation given at Baptism. To start your thinking, read if you like Luke 5:1-11, the Call of the First Disciples.

Is such a commitment for me? What would it involve?

(To those who feel they have already made such a decision, this meeting comes only as an invitation to renew and deepen its joy, and increase its force for vibrant Christian living. And if some other commitment than the two mentioned above would be more appropriate, read Meditations 3-7 below in that light.)

3. Is Any Commitment to Jesus for Me—Now?

Is He inviting, like the Lover in The Song of Songs 2:10-13? Or as He invited the young man in Mark 10:17-22? (Read.)

If wondering about it, take the Gospels. Open and read. Does this Man attract, fascinate you? Are you inclined to say, "Yes, I'm yours. Own me. Use me. Live in me. I love you. I'm putting myself and everything else in your hands!"?

"Come: Live in my heart and pay no rent."
—*Samuel Lover*

Are you inclined to make a commitment to at least some form of prayer-contact, "from now and forever?" Is such a commitment possible? Is it wise? What if I change my mind?

As you read this meditation, ask if any dialogue, or wrestling with God, is going on in your life over issues like these. If not, 'tis almost a pity—pray that one starts! "Behold, I stand at the door and knock."

---

4. Motivation for Commitment.

Most good people at one time or another feel moved toward dedicating themselves to God, finding Jesus, giving themselves to Him, accepting Him, or however they put it.

To outside appearances it may look like life as usual. But interiorly, because of the love involved, the difference is night and day. It's the difference between saints and those who don't think much about God, Jesus, or the Kingdom from one Sunday to the next. St. Theresa, for example, who died when she was only 24, knew that from the divine point of view the greatness of an act (in the realms of grace and good accomplished) is in the greatness of the love that animates it. She'd "offer up" the annoyance of being splashed repeatedly by the sister carelessly doing dishes beside her. For Theresa, this was opportunity to love. Small things, done with great love, become great. She was named co-patron of the Missions for the Universal Church (with Francis Xavier) though she never preached, or baptized anyone!

This is an invitation. Are you one who is ready for some kind of commitment? Should any commitment be considered? Matthew 19:27-30 suggests advantages . . . if you are ready. See also Luke 21: 1-4 about little things becoming great.

---

5. The Feel of It.

In your mind's eye try to imagine the feel of some kind of definite commitment to Jesus. Would you somehow feel more peace? If so, a positive sign. If not, you may not be ready.

No least advantage to commitment to the Lord is the sense of closer union with Him. It's finding Jesus. He's yours. You're His. It adds meaning to life. Each day the commitment is lived is a good day. You are His disciple. So you surmount somewhat more easily human frustrations and coldness for you live not as much for success—or even for return of human love—as for Him. And, as long as you have Him, you've Someone to live for—even if things aren't going so well. You have Him for a friend, who, if others leave, never will He. Even if you offend by sin and so leave Him—never will He refuse your overtures to return—even seventy times seven. One can live life with zest each day—because each is a day of love. Somehow, everything's better.

This is the invitation. Are you one who is ready for some kind of commitment? Will you ever be? What is the kind of saint you can be? What is the unique way of following Jesus with zest and enthusiasm that is your own? (Saint: one who loves God and man extraordinarily well.) Would you find joy? Consider it if you like against Matthew 11:28-30. Or if the decision is difficult, against John 16:20-22 and Matthew 16:24-27.

6. Testimonies of the Committed.

a) "I don't know who or what put the question. I don't know when it was put. I don't even remember answering. But at some moment I did answer "Yes" to Someone or Something, and from that hour I was certain that existence is meaningful, and that therefore, my life in self-surrender had a goal."
—Dag Hammarskjold, Sec'y-General to the United Nations, shortly before his plane-crash death.

b) "I feel I'm going through life with a friend. It sure beats going alone. . . ." (age 29)

c) "My guilt is gone. . . . . It's sort of like being in love and the sun's out and the birds are singing
. . . . and I know it sounds crazy
. . . . but life is different." (19)

A few others:
"I've been looking for something like this . . . .
Now life has meaning . . . . not some thing
. . . . but some One!" (46)

"Thou hast made us for Thyself O Lord, and
we are restless till we rest in Thee."
—St. Augustine

"O Beauty, ever ancient ever new!
Too little and too late have I loved Thee!"
—St. Augustine

7. The Mass: An Invitation to Join Jesus in Commitment to the Father

The Mass can be regarded as Christ's invitation to join Him in offering ourselves in total commitment to the will of our Father.

At Mass Christ renews the offering of the commitment to His Father which he lived out all through his life and completed on Calvary. This was the commitment to do His Father's will for the sake of the Kingdom, cost what it might. (This, more than His suffering, was the love-act that redeemed us.)

But Christ offers Himself at Mass not only as Jesus alone, but as Christ-the-Head-of His-Mystical-Body. Christ offers Himself as Head and members, and those members happen to be you and me. We are being offered with Christ to the Father at every Mass whether we know it or not.

What is *being offered* supposed to mean? It is supposed to mean the same for us as it meant for Christ: total willingness to do our Father's will for the sake of the Kingdom. It's as if Jesus says at the moment of the Consecration: "I'm now renewing the offering of my Body and Blood to the Father to save the world. Since you are my members I am offering you too, your body and blood as well as mine, to do the same. In other words I want your help—whoever you are and at whatever place in life you are—to redeem the world and bring all persons to the fullness of life in the Kingdom. Of course to make this offering meaningful, you must agree. . . ."

What we should be doing then at Mass is just that—agreeing to offer ourselves with Him. Otherwise His offering of us lacks some of the meaning it could have, and the Mass (on our part) gives less honor and love to God and is less efficacious for the needs of all of us than it could be.

All this begins at the Offertory. Bringing to the altar the bread and wine is supposed to symbolize bringing *ourselves* under this form of bread and wine. They are the "work of our hands." They stand for our body and blood—ourselves. In former times people made the very bread and wine they offered. Now we substitute money as a more convenient way to do the same thing.

Then at the time of Consecration, the bread and wine become the Body and Blood of Christ. However the bread and wine still represent ourselves too, so the symbolism is that we, for whom they continue to stand, should be becoming Christ too. We are to do so—not physically, obviously—but by becoming as much like Him as we can in mind and heart, in acting like He did out of love, and for the same goals: "Thy Kingdom come; Thy Will be done."

Notice that the bread and wine are consecrated separately. This can remind us that we are being invited to offer ourselves in commitment that is total, all of ourselves, even to death if need be. The double consecration, signifying the separation of body and blood, and therefore death, is the sacramental form in which Christ is offered again in every Mass to the Father. We—still represented by these same two species—are being offered to the Father with Christ in the same way—being invited to "go all the way," being invited to become dead to ourselves that we may live for Christ in whatever form this may take in our lives.

The Offertory is only preparation. We are *actually* offered by Christ to the Father through the hands of the priest in the words of the Eucharistic Prayer immediately following the Consecration when the priest says: "Father . . . calling to mind Christ's Passion, etc. . . . we (Christ and ourselves) offer you this holy and living sacrifice (Christ and ourselves, head and members) . . ." The Fourth Eucharistic Prayer states our involvement even more pointedly: "Father . . . gather all who share this bread and wine into the one body of Christ, a living sacrifice of praise . . ." At these words we should be making the same offering. At the end of the Eucharistic Prayer we can reaffirm our assent as we say "Amen" (The "Great Amen"), and reaffirm it once more in the Our Father: "Thy Kingdom come; Thy will be done."

At Communion Jesus comes as a return gift, giving of Himself in return for our giving of ourselves to Him. And He comes to strengthen us to live out the offering, and to unite in love and mutual support the other members of His Body He has invited to make the same offering.

Would that everyone could feel this challenge to go all out for Christ-and-the-Kingdom when he or she attends Mass. In view of the practical implications and perhaps the "wrestling with God" involved, our weekly Mass (viewed as an invitation to pledge ourselves to whole-hearted living for God for the week to come) could hardly be boring! One grieves to see people attending Mass in a passive or disinterested way, hoping it will be short, etc. Mass can also serve as renewal time for any commitment decided on in Meditations 1-6 above. It is also a fine opportunity to hearten ourselves once again for the daily battle of trying to do His will one day at a time, and to live one day at a time committed to the people and the work the Lord would have us committed to for the sake of the Kingdom.

8-9-10:

Reread and consider any of the above meditations; or read St. Mark on the Passion of Our Lord with a view to loving Jesus more or strengthening your resolution of commitment.

Suggested sequence:
    Med. 8 Mark 14:1-42
    Med. 9 Mark 14:43 to 15:20
    Med. 10 Mark 15:21-41

I can do all things—more than I think—
in Him who strengthens me,
especially when it is quite clear that
this
is the job, situation, role, joy or sorrow
He wants me to manage.

Perhaps the biggest reason people fail to grow
to a certain spiritual maturity,
or to Become or Do something Great,
Is:

they just Don't Think they can do it.
And if they are trying to go it alone, they just may be right.

MEETING
14
BETTER PRAYER AMID THE HUSTLE AND BUSTLE

Meditations 1-5 Finding God by Using Our Senses

1. Ears.

Listen to a song or music. Try praying over what you hear.

2. Eyes.

Look at a picture. Study it. Gaze. Let it fascinate you. Is *He* somehow to be found in portraits, or real people? In photographs—or real nature?

3. People in Action.

Watch one or several persons in action—whether by TV, photo, or just out the window. Could something about the persons or what they are doing lead one to prayer?

4. Reading or Study.

Read an article—in a newspaper, magazine or textbook. Attempt somehow to pray over its contents. Is the front page a "Prayer-book?" How might you find Him in "Newsweek?" History or Science? A Novel?

5. Sense of Beauty or Feeling of Pleasure.

Read some poetry. Or contemplate an art object: some "thing of beauty (which) is a joy forever." Read or look at it as if for the first time. Could it lead to prayer? For example, "If this be so attractive—how much must He."

This is a grand way to pray during travel, or at a concert.

Alternate Meditation. Eat a meal alone—with Him.

Meditations 6-9. Finding God in Your Own Way. Styles in the Spiritual Life.

There are many "spiritual styles"—ways people relate to God and pray. Some clues to finding your own are:

Your temperament and inclinations,
Listening for the Lord's leading,
Noting what brings most peace of soul,
Special needs, faults, or trials that need attention,
The circumstances you are in,
The role and work God has given you.

Use the meditations below to think about your style, get acquainted with others and prepare to experiment in the months ahead.

---

6. General Styles are those based on an overall attitude toward God and how best to relate to Him. They express a basic spiritual stance toward God and life.

a) "The Little Way." Spiritual childhood. Everything is in the hands of

Our Father. We trust Him absolutely, and give ourselves to Him—and accept everything as coming from Him.

b) The "Divine Milieu." God is everywhere—mirrored in His beautiful qualities (attributes, "footsteps") or saving activity in people, nature, and the events of life.

"The heavens show forth . . . ."

c) All for Jesus. All for the glory of God. Do everything for Him. Make and renew the Morning Offering.

d) Love people. Christ is in everyone, so *love them.* "Do all the good you can." And always be kind—always.

e) Compassion. Acts for and listens to the poor, sick, lonely, retarded, aged . . . . as in Matthew 25:31-46.

f) The Kingdom. "*Do* something about the way things are. . . ." Preaches or works actively for justice, peace, relief of hunger, etc.

g) "Be ye perfect." Takes great care with ordinary matters and tries hard to do each one well for the Lord.

h) "Be human." Let the humanity of Jesus shine through you as well as you can—in everything. "Be Christlike."

i) Awareness of one's role and dignity. "I am a certain kind of person: a Christian; and that's all I need to know." I think, judge and act accordingly.

j) Others: Avoiding sin; pervading gratitude for being saved; finding God-in-others in community living; withdrawing from the world; sense of humbleness before His greatness—or combinations of the above. Each has its merits. Which ones appeal to you most? Do you have a "style"?

---

7. **During-the-Day Styles. Helpful while "on-the-run."**

a) "Instant" prayers—short, informal. "Dear Lord . . . ."

b) "Visits." Short periods of withdrawal. Scheduled or snatched.

c) Repeat-prayers. Mantra-like—like a sweet refrain running through the head and heart, such as ejaculations, psalm verses, or the Jesus Prayer: "Lord Jesus, Son of God, Have Mercy on Me." Make up your own "mantra."

d) Frequent renewals of Intention. "This is for you Lord—I hope you will like it."

e) Recalling His nearness and presence—like a lover not far in his thoughts from the joy of his life.

f) Formal prayers said at fixed hours, for example, the layman's office or the rosary.

g) One long definite, quiet period of prayer every day. One looks forward to it all during the day and saves up material . . .

h) Praying over the everyday. Take life as it comes and pray out of the interests and stuff of the moment—anytime, many times—all through the day. (Recommended.)

i) Listening. One attends frequently to the voice of the Spirit, asking for leads and guidance.

j) Recollection of a favorite truth or loving thought: "The love of Christ urges me." "Christ died for me."

k) Recall of one's meditation. Recommended.

l) Repeating some petition for help . . . for example, "Help me become one who . . . ."

M) Longing. Awareness of one's restlessness and feeling of inner emptiness—with longing for Him to fill it.

What is your style if you have one?
Experiment freely.
Which of the above do you like?

8. Time-Together Styles. Intimate Prayer in times set aside.

a) Use a book. Read slowly—aloud if possible. Linger where you find profit. Don't move on till the well runs dry. (This is one of the most generally helpful of all prayer methods.)

b) Think-Talk-Act. Think about what the passage or its phrases mean or imply. Talk with the Lord about it. Consider action.

c) Free-flowing conversation with the Lord—heart to Heart—about whatever comes to mind. If nothing comes, simply listen—remain quietly in His presence until something does.

d) Repeat phrases, Psalm verses, etc., over and over—enjoying, resting, in the mood they suggest.

e) Yoga: Repetition of prayers, phrases or "praises" coordinated with rhythmic breathing and body movements.

f) Write the meditation or draw it. "Meditate with a pencil." Or read it aloud dramatically.

g) Imagination. Be there. See it all happen. Feel for—and with—one of the persons involved. Then reflect on how you yourself might feel if you were there.

h) Read or sing portions of the Divine Office or other prayers slowly and thoughtfully. Concentrate on saying the prayers well.

i) Use music, art, poetry or scene from nature (As in Med. 1-5 above.) Variations: Pray while attending a concert or art museum. Or combine your prayer with hiking, skiing, swimming, surfing, biking, or some other enjoyable activity or hobby you do alone. (Think about this one!)

j) Simply remain attentive to His presence in quiet, the mind fixed on Him, or on His goodness or happiness, or beauty. Or: on a scene from Scripture—which you behold like the angels with wondering awe . . . .

k) Examination of Conscience: My life: What is going on? What kind of person am I becoming? Am I growing? "Will it matter that I was?"

l) Prayer over our times, the good and evil occurring whether in darkest Africa, the neighborhood school or the latest in crises.

m) Prolonged periods of quiet "listening."

n) Remaining humbly before Him with open hands, sensing one's emptiness, or inability to pray, love or respond.

---

9. Group-Prayer Possibilities.

a) Liturgical—Why not consider daily Mass once or more during the week?

b) Charismatic or other prayer groups. Visit one. It might suit your inclination. You lose nothing by a visit.

c) Shared Prayer. Read a passage. Reflect silently. Then any who wish may offer reactions or thoughts. Then silence again. Then prayer in the form of direct address: "Father, we see from this reading . . . ."
A gentle method which appeals to many.

d) Faith sharing. Variation of the above. Pick a certain topic, doctrine, virtue, or event in Scripture—even the name "God," and pool notions about what it means. Hear from each in turn with no pressure to participate. "To me, Religion means . . . ."

e) Free-flow. Everyone brings something to a meeting and shares it—a favorite prayer, reading, or recent experience. Discuss or pray about it as moved.

f) Study courses, Bible courses, programs in the spiritual life (such as this), spiritual book reviews, courses in Theology or the Social Encyclicals, and human relations workshops—may all have good potential for furnishing prayer material.

g) One could also consider the Quaker style: simply gathering together and remaining in quiet—each person centering deeply on God.

10. Planning.

Spend this meditation preparing and praying for our next and last meeting. Prepare suggestions or questions for discussion. Have you found any books you could recommend as follow-up spiritual reading? What should we do next year? Who, besides ourselves, will benefit from our work?

> Earth's crammed with heaven,
> And every common bush afire with God,
> And only he who sees
> takes off his shoes.
> The rest sit round it
> and pluck blackberries.
> —*E. B. Browning*

PROGRESS IN PRAYER

Prayer is basically attending to God. It has many forms: from active thinking and conversation, to quieter repetition of some favorite phrase, to simply remaining in speechless awe and praise before Him.

As you continue in prayer, let one of your efforts be to try to become increasingly aware of what the Spirit may be prompting in the inner reaches of your soul. To do so, wait quietly and patiently after a reading, allowing the mind and heart to become open to whatever is occurring within. If some response seems to occur, follow this lead in your prayer.

For example when examining your conscience, rather than thinking about virtues and vices, or thoughts, words and deeds, simply unravel your life, let the past day or week unwind before Him. Then quietly wait to see what movements of soul, what responses for prayer or suggestions for change come to mind. When you read Scripture, instead of asking many questions or making comparisons—though at times these may be useful—first allow the passage to produce its own effect, quietly opening yourself to letting it—or the Spirit—work on you. And when contemplating nature—let your heart rise to Him who is its source, and standing as it were interiorly before Him, there praise and admire. Do not stop short at mere enjoyment of the object, music or scene.

Sometimes stirring of soul will not occur, for prayer is God's gift and may be offered or not at His good pleasure. We on our part, as some one observed, do what we can to make prayer happen, and then stand back to see if it will. But if no sense of God's closeness, nor any reaction occurs, do not cease from prayer. Just do what you can—whatever feels right. Read a little further, or re-read the first passage more thoughtfully. There is much to be said for just reading, waiting for response, and reflecting; and then continuing again to read, wait and think or respond as one can. This generosity and faithfulness to prayer is quite pleasing to God.

Do not clutter prayer with too many thoughts or questions. Prefer depth of insight and appreciation if such is available. Thus the prayer direction about lingering where one finds profit, and remaining with the insight or sense of his presence is a valuable one.

If at times you feel drawn to almost wordless prayer, to simply remaining before Him in quiet and peace, in admiration, or some other affection, or to quietly contemplating some scene in Scripture, know that this is good prayer. Feel free to remain with it as long as the attraction lasts.

Sometimes all one can do is stand before God with open and empty hands, hardly knowing what to say, feeling the weight of one's littleness, powerlessness, and inability to pray. This too is good prayer.

At the same time, if you do not feel drawn to more interior prayer, but feel that it helps you most to analyze text, to think about and apply it to your life, or to converse with the Lord as moved, by all means continue to do so. This too is good prayer and may be best for you at this particular time. Let the Spirit lead.

One could summarize much of the above by saying that one of the most universally acceptable, easy and profitable methods for mental prayer—if one has to make a choice—is that of Sacred Reading. "Sacred reading" means to read a spiritual book such as Scripture or that of some author who has unction and power to lift the spirit; then pause wherever you find fruit, profit, or insight for reflection. When the attraction or your ability to pray over the passage gives out, or when distractions occur, go back to reading again. On a "dry" day you will read much and pray little. On a day of consolations in prayer you will pray much and read little—but you will profit either way.

The monks of the desert knew sacred reading as their only set form of prayer and would often follow these steps in order: (1) *read*, (2) *reflect*, question, (3) *pray*, talk, communicate, express feelings and respond, (4) *contemplate* quietly. Modern authors would suggest—as we have done throughout this course—interposing a period of interior listening before reflecting or praying. Allow yourself to become aware of interior response and if one occurs follow that lead. One may float back and forth between these activities in any way one is inclined.

A few notes: You will pray better during longer periods if you try to cultivate brief prayer-contacts during the day; and if you try to seek His will during the day even in the smaller choices to be made. You will be helped also in longer periods by the inspiration of spiritual books and the advice and helps of a spiritual director.

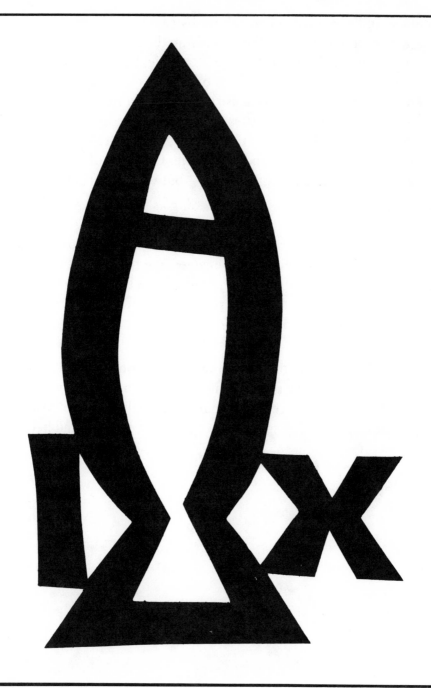

15

BETTER PRAYER: THE ROLE OF THE SPIRIT, AND PLANNING FOR GROWTH.

Meditations

1. Two Presences of the Spirit. *Read Acts 2:1-4*

Think long and deeply about how Jesus did not leave us orphans (John 14:18) but dwells with us in His Spirit, especially in His Church. Let yourself feel the comfort and trust His presence affords.

He is also present in the interior of our souls as in a temple (1 Cor. 3:16). Explore in prayer what dignity this presence gives each person, and its implications for respect for life and avoidance of violence. This presence is also the basis for His constant communication with each of us (Romans 8:14-16; 26-27). But . . . .we must listen!

2. The Spirit of Guidance and Power. *Read John 16:12-13 and Acts 2:1-4*

God the Holy Spirit is creatively involved with human life. After the Resurrection, He came as a mighty force, affording Light and Courage to speak and witness to the Good News. Do you need more Light or more Courage? (For being and acting like Christians, not everyone will love us.) Whither is He leading you, me, the Church, the world today? How does one know?

3. Community and Unity-Forming Action. *Two outstanding texts are Acts 2:42-47 and 4:32-35*

Should the Church be showing itself more a community? Are the early

121

Christians a model for our day? How much and what kind of community are people looking for?

---

4. **The Fruits of the Spirit.** *See Galatians 5:22-23 and 1 Thessalonians 5:16-18*

   St. Augustine says of a Christian that he is an Alleluia from the crown of his head to the tips of his toes.

   Is that possible—life being what it is?

   Also: What is the place of praise of God in the life of the Christian?

---

5. **Distribution of Gifts.** *Read 1 Corinthians 12:4-7*

   Paul says our gifts and talents are for the building up of His Body, especially the Church.

   How many look at their gifts this way?

   Talk with the Lord as moved.

---

6. **20 Tips to Improve Prayer.** (*Last page.*) *Read them slowly while "listening" for what applies to yourself.*

---

7. **A Summary of the Course:** *Read Mark 12:28-34a*

   Christians are lovers,
   followers of Jesus in the work of His Kingdom,
   children of our Father, and
   led by His Spirit.

Christians live
one day at a time, trying to
love God with all their minds and hearts,
health and money, talents and crosses—as well as they can—
and their neighbors as themselves
that His Kingdom may come.
    "Thy will be done; Thy Kingdom come."

They are buoyed up
by the promise of eternal life,
and so, prayerfully and lovingly, they serve the Lord and
all people—the poor and neglected especially—
    until He comes.

---

8. Planning for Growth. Your Prayer Life.

What are you really going to do about spiritual living—and about prayer-practices in particular—for the future?

---

9. Planning for Growth. In Your Parish.

Read Galatians 6:9-10 and consider the closeness of your ties to your local "household of faith:" your parish.

Do you see any ways you might
"Do good" as St. Paul commends?
Consider talking with your pastor
about opportunities.

---

10. Planning for Growth. In the Church.

Consider your involvement with Christ's Church today—for an extended period of days as you read *Acts of the Apostles* (all of it if you can). It concerns especially the work of Peter and Paul.

(*Read the Introductory Notes in your Bible for background.*)

Try to admire the spirit and the zeal of these men. What did they do, and what were their motives? What did you learn about the Church? Does it make you proud of your membership?

Do the chapters suggest anything about your participation in her life and goals?

> *Remember:* We are the Church.

Planning for Growth—Some Suggestions.

Good follow-ups for this course would be the continuing practice of slow, thought-and-prayer-filled reading of Scripture or some good spiritual book; of Scripture, perhaps a chapter a day; of books, perhaps one on prayer, the spiritual life, or lives of saints.

This practice would furnish material for prayer, and hopefully educate and inspire as well. Consider assembling a short book-list for everyone.

Consider attending a course in Scripture, meeting with others for prayer or Bible-study, or taking *PRAY* again.

In a more active way, consider deeper involvement with your parish, the Church or volunteer activities.

Consider also the apostolate of *PRAY*: teaching the course or getting others acquainted.

A few recommended books:

The Making of a Saint—Kreyche—Alba House.
A guide to the spiritual life.

Christ in the Gospel—Fr. Frey—Confraternity Publications.
A pocket harmony for daily meditation.

(*You and your Moderator may suggest others.*)

For Discussion

The highest form of love is: to share with others the best of what we have: life—courage—vision—faith—the knowledge and love of Jesus Christ.

What should we do next year?
Do you know of books you'd recommend?
What will be the fruit of our year's work? Who will benefit?
Is there anything we can do to support or promote prayer (or *PRAY*), or the coming of the Kingdom—or knowing and loving: Jesus?

May the road rise to meet you
May the wind be always at your back
May the sun shine warm upon your face
And the rains fall soft upon your fields,
And, until we meet again,
May God hold you in the palm of His hand!
—*Gaelic Prayer*

---

20 TIPS TO IMPROVE PRAYERS

Prayer requires these things: Discipline, fidelity, seclusion and rhythm. Two tools consistently needed: Discipline and will power. "We are free (in prayer) only if we are patterned."

These, the conclusions of hundreds of prayerful people who have synthesized their experience and are willing to share it with the *PRAY* readers. Here are tips, suggestions, ideas out of today's modern experience, as synthesized by Sister Annette Boyle, IHM.

If you want to be successful at prayer, you must have a "definite time." If you don't have one, the prayer conclusions say, "you select it."

Also emerging strongly: Getting into prayer, a living vibrant prayer, helps you learn a lot about yourself. The conclusions note: "My mood affects me and may color the way I pray, but, they add, it does not affect God's saving action." So to pray well, first "Become aware of your mood: tired, depressed, lazy, joyful, peaceful, distracted."

Suggested:

- You can control the mood. . . .
    silence helps
- You can give the time, attention,
    desire
- You can ask the grace of confidence
    in the process.

"Prayer is the openness to all reality, the work of the Spirit in us, but we must cooperate and dispose ourselves, as much as possible."

"In our struggle to be ourselves, we have our best prayer."
1) Jesus gives us the friendship—not that we deserve or earn it but that we need. In our need is a new covenant found?

2) It is not our unworthiness that keeps us from the Lord, but our unwillingness to see and accept that unworthiness . . . . Allow God to be your redeemer."

What you are doing while you pray also affects your prayer. "Take a relaxing and meaningful position." What does this mean? It means knowing yourself well enough to realize that some ways of sitting, kneeling, standing, etc., may be more conducive for your prayer than others. So if you pray best sitting, sit. If you have found some of the traditional eastern prayer positions (practiced in yoga or zen) to be helpful, do that. If you pray best kneeling, kneel. Know what is best for you and act accordingly when you pray.

Some other tips:

- Pause when something strikes
    you—because the Spirit may be speaking
    to you in a special way.
- Pause if you experience the Lord's presence,
    His love:

1) If you are moved to express yourself in a special way.

2) If you are peaceful.

3) If something disturbs or even repels you. The Lord may speak here also.

4) If you feel lifted up by the Spirit.

Scripture as an aid to prayer cannot be overlooked. These are suggested ways to approach and savor scripture-based prayer:

- Read a passage slowly. Ask yourself questions about it, for example, "In the early morning Jesus went away by Himself to pray." Ask: Who? Where? Why? How? What?

- Read and ponder three or four texts of the same incident using Matthew, Mark, Luke and John.

- Take one text and deepen it. Gaze on the text to come to different levels of involvement. For example, in the Storm at Sea incident:

1st level: See externals, see boats, waves, people.
2nd level: See details, Jesus asleep disciples frightened.
3rd level: See yourself there, use your imagination, be present in the mystery, look at the persons, hear the Apostles, Jesus speak. Be one of the Apostles. Respond. Ask the Lord for what you need.

The following are 20 tips you can apply to prayer.

As you begin:

1. Find a suitable place—free from distractions.

2. Realize that harmony of body and spirit is important. Take a peaceful, relaxed position.

3. Spend a few moments quieting yourself—come into the presence of the Lord—believing He is with you.

4. Ask for the grace you most desire.

5. Read slowly the Scripture passage.

6. Pause where you feel drawn.

7. Ponder it as Mary did.

8. With your heart respond to it.

To see how you have spent your prayer time

1. What passage did I choose?

2. What grace did I ask for?

3. What was my mood, changes in mood?

4. Where did I dwell?

5. What was enjoyable? distasteful?

6. What did the Lord teach me?

7. Was I faithful to the time of prayer?

To look at your spiritual growth

1. Ask for the light of the Holy Spirit to know—

2. How am I experiencing being drawn by the Father to Himself?

   How my sinful nature is tempting me, turning me from the Father?

3. Thank the Lord for the ways in which He has been present and I have been able to respond to His love.

4. Ask forgiveness for the times I have not responded to His love.

5. Trust that He will be with me.

5 YEARS' EXPERIENCE

These "prayer tips" are the result of 5 years' worth of research and experimentation that developed from the summer House of Prayer Experience (HOPE) sessions sponsored by the Monroe (Mich.) Immaculate Heart of Mary Sisters. Participants in the 6 weeks of prayerful, contemplative living for active apostolate Sisters contributed their ideas, criticism, suggestions and discoveries of prayer. These feedback ideas were synthesized and edited by IHM Sister Annette Boyle who gave permission to the Crux of *PRAYER* to share them with its readers.